T H E

BELIEF SYSTEM

the Secret to Motivation and Improved Performance

*Unleash the power
of motivation
by tr̶i̶g̶g̶e̶r̶i̶n̶g̶
three very* **fs**

D1377518

Thad Green, Ph.D. and Merwyn Hayes, Ph.D.

BEECHWOOD PRESS
Winston-Salem, NC

Library of Congress Cataloging-in-Publication Data

Green, Thad, and Merwyn Hayes

The Belief System : the secret to motivation and improved
performance / Thad Green and Merwyn Hayes.

ISBN 0-9640040-0-3

Library of Congress Catalog Card Number: 93-91860
ISBN: 0-9640040-0-3

First published in 1994
Second Printing in 2003

Beechwood Press, Winston-Salem, NC

Printed in the United States of America

Acknowledgement

We want to thank Bill Barkley and AT&T for providing the proving grounds for The Belief System of Motivation and Performance.

Preface

The Belief System™ and The Belief System of Motivation And Performance™ are the trademarks of Thad B. Green, Ph.D. Dr. Green's creation, a work in progress since 1977, is the subject of this book.

A Special Thanks

We especially want to express our appreciation to John Thompson who took two diverse writing styles and blended them into a product that pleases us both.

When the Belief System of Motivation And Performance walks in your door, it says, "Give the organization's motivation and performance problems to your employees to solve. They know better than anyone else what's bothering them, and they know what will remedy the situation. *Just ask them . . . .*" And they will show you how it's done.

When the prospects for accomplishing this settles in, you will get excited. Very excited. Image the gain in performance your organization could achieve if employees became systematically involved in solving their own motivation and performance problems. The trick as a manager is to understand what motivates people. Unfortunately, it is more than offering rewards. The *Belief System* will help you understand.

After you sit through the first training session with your direct-reports, you may want to get *everyone* trained in the Belief System. Not just managers, but everyone. A program has been devised that will cascade the *Belief System* down through the organization, a program that will stick. Performance management cannot be forced. No motivation training is going to improve performance if the people it is designed to motivate elect not to use the training. In our opinion, this is the single biggest problem in management development today.

The Belief System has gone far in changing the way many organizations do business by improving the motivation and performance of the people in them. The impact of the Belief System tends to exceed every one of management's expectations.

-Thad Green
-Merwyn Hayes

Contents

Introduction

Motivation is the spark that ignites *performance* in human endeavors from love to sports to business to art to religion and more. Yet, few people understand the dynamics of the one to the other. With this book, we would help you to better understand motivation so that you might reap the bounty of heightened performance. Let us first introduce each other.

Merwyn Hayes:

Thad Green is the foremost authority on motivation in America today. That is my studied opinion. Thad would never say it, he is inordinately modest; I can say it with considerable confidence. There is not much that has been written or said on the subject of motivation and performance in the last 30 years that I have not become familiar with. And no one has put theory into practice with the practical effectiveness Thad has achieved with the Belief System Of Motivation And Performance.

INTRODUCTION

I am proud of my nurturing role in the development of the Belief System, but it is a product born of Thad Green. In 1976, after delving into the work of Victor Vroom of Yale University, he saw the missing links in the popular theories of motivation. More importantly, he saw a chance to re-make theory into an effective tool of the managerial profession and, in so doing, change for the better the lives of managers and employees alike. Thad went to work re-conceptionalizing Vroom's findings so they could be better understood in the workplace. Concurrently, he carefully crafted the application model that would set his work apart from other theorists in the management field. What emerged put decades of scholarly findings by the best minds in motivation research into the hands of working managers who seek simply to improve the performance of their employees.

Thad's first book, *Performance And Motivation Strategies For Today's Workforce* (Quorum, 1992), is the "bible" of Belief System theory and application. *The Belief System*, condenses the first and breaks ground with its "user-friendly" approach to manager-employee training. It is a pleasure for me to be a part of this product.

THE BELIEF SYSTEM

Thad Green:

Merwyn is a man of substance and achievement who has made his mark high on the wall of managerial communications. For two decades, he has stood at the top of the consulting profession in matters of "team development and executive coaching." The role of persuasion and influencing in modern management practice has taken on entirely new dimensions with Merwyn's tutelage. Major corporations at home and abroad avail themselves of his expertise, as have professional and collegiate athletic teams, universities of the ilk of Harvard and Wake Forest and operations like The Power Station, "the worlds best recording studio," owned in part by the Bongiovi (Bon Jovi) family.

The Hayes Group International was started by Merwyn 27 years ago, serving at this point in history over 1200 organizations around the world. It has become a premier organization in serving clients in the fields of executive coaching, change management, and team development.

Friends since 1974, this, then, is the fellow who came to me and the Belief System at a propitious time. At 40 years of age, I had taken my expertise into the marketplace in search of riches and, as fortune would have it, found what I was looking for. Financially secure, I retired. *With Performance And Motivation Strategies For Today's Workforce*, I fully expected to retire the Belief System to that musky

INTRODUCTION

corner of the public library reserved for long forgotten management tomes. At least I had captured for those who might seek it out what I knew was a superb instrument of employee motivation, tried and tempered in the work-a-day world. The Belief System had served me well but, content in retirement, I was not prepared to do more with it. Then along came Merwyn with the impetus. He embraced the Belief System and stirred in me an excitement about passing on the methodology. In large part, this book is a product of Merwyn's enthusiasm for the Belief System. Those who find benefit in its precepts owe him a substantial vote of thanks.

Since the first printing of this book in 1993, much has happened. The Belief System of Motivation and Performance has been widely used in a variety of organizations. Of particular interest is its application in large and small sales organizations, as described in *Developing and Leading the Sales Organization* (Quorum Books, 1998).

We trust that all who read this book, *The Belief System*, will gain a broader perspective of what motivation truly is, specifically that it is more than offering rework and striving for employee satisfaction, much more. In the nine years since the original printing of this book, "It's simple!" is what people say, and it's back now.

CHAPTER 1

The Offering Is Never Enough

Modern management strategies relating to employee motivation and performance are rooted in theories that say, in essence, "offer people something they want as incentive to perform and they will work hard to get it." Only trouble is, as any seasoned manager will tell you, the theories don't always work. Did you ever fail to see the satisfaction in an "all-expenses-paid, three-day cruise" when all you wanted for your performance was a raise? Have you ever been offered a bonus for a performance level you knew was impossible to achieve? How motivated were you to chase that reward? Were you ever party to a reward offered but never delivered? What happened the *next* time that reward was held out as incentive to perform well? No takers? Where is the motivation in a father's offer of a new car to an academically deficient son if he makes the dean's list next semester? Think about it: how many times are people offered attractive rewards that fail to result in the effort and performance necessary to get them? It happens all too frequently. Why is this?

That is a question that has occupied the authors of this book throughout our respective careers, first as university professors, then as consultants and successful hands-on businessmen. The trouble with popular theories of motivation, including those by the likes of Abraham Maslow and Frederick Herzberg, is that they don't translate well to the realities of the workplace. Specifically, the motivation theories in wide use today are *incomplete*, they proceed from a single truth when there are three; and they come with *no practical guide for utilization.* Theory rarely holds form under pressure to shape it into a useful tool of production.

The **Belief System Of Motivation And Performance** changes that. It is a historical step forward in the imperfect art and science of human motivation. With this book, we hope to convey to employers a vital, simple truth: what employees *believe* is infinitely more important than what is being *offered* by management to motivate them.

The Chain Of Beliefs

The Belief System explains how people determine (1) how hard they will work and (2) how well they

THE OFFERING IS NEVER ENOUGH

will perform. These decisions spring from a process or chain of events that goes like this: *effort* leads to *performance* which leads to *outcomes* (e.g., a promotion, a raise, a pat on the back, etc.) which results in *satisfaction* (or dissatisfaction). An employee's effort can be a little or a lot, resulting in performance that is good or bad, begetting outcomes big or small that produce high or low levels of satisfaction or dissatisfaction. Whatever the variables, the principle remains the same.

Effort ⟶ Performance ⟶ Outcomes ⟶ Satisfaction

The popular theories of motivation focus solely on the end of the process—the relationship between *outcomes* and *satisfaction*. The way to motivate employees, according to these theories, is to offer them something they want and they will work hard to get it. (The other side of this tactic is to offer employees something they *don't* want— unemployment, perhaps—and they will work hard to avoid getting it.)

Effort ⟶ Performance ⟶ Outcomes ⟶ Satisfaction

> Offer employees what they want, and they will work hard to get it . . . or, offer them what they don't want, and they will work hard *not* to get it.

The problem with simply offering employees

something they want (desirable outcomes) as inducement to work harder and perform better is that part of the basic equation is ignored; the product that follows is happenstance. The Belief System does not dispute the importance of offering employees what they want, it just points out that the *offering* alone is not enough.

Employees must first *believe* certain specific things before the offering of desirable outcomes produces the motivation managers desire and expect. The beliefs, three in all, are the key to motivating employees, and all three must be "believed" or motivation suffers and everyone loses to some extent or another.

The First Belief
"Can I do it?"

The first belief (Belief-1) deals with the relationship between employee *effort* and *performance*. What must be believed is that one's effort will lead to performance. If there is not this belief, there is a motivation problem, perhaps a big one. Consciously or unconsciously, people will always ask themselves, "If I give it my best, will the effort lead to the performance desired? Can I do it?" in other words. (The belief may be expressed as a question, "Can I do it?" or as a positive, "Yes, I can do it," or as a negative, "No, I can't do it.")

Suppose a person is offered something very desirable but concludes, "I can't do the job." When people say to themselves, "I really want that outcome, but no matter how hard I try, I can't perform well enough to get it," what happens to motivation? Obviously, it suffers. It happens in corporate downsizing when jobs are combined and heaped on overworked employees. It happens when sales or production quotas are raised to improbable levels. It happens when people are placed in positions of responsibility when they do not have the necessary training or experience. Even though employees in situations like these may be offered *something they want,* outcomes they believe will be satisfying, motivation does not result simply because it is believed, "I can't do it" (Belief-1). People must believe that the effort they are capable of giving will be sufficient to perform as expected.

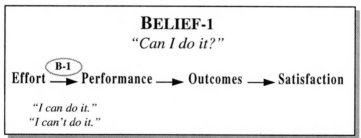

Belief-1 problems are pervasive in today's workplace. Unfortunately, they usually go undetected, principally because people don't find them easy to talk about. Why? People generally don't like to confess their shortcomings. It's human nature. In the minds of many, there are feelings of inadequacy and weakness attached to such admissions; so people usually don't make them. The problems are covered up.

Not only do people tend to cover up Belief-1 problems, they even deny their existence, lie about them. So it is that as consultants we often hear, "Sure, I can do it," when the truth turns out to be quite the opposite. Why? Fear of the consequences. "If the boss thinks I can't do the job, he'll find someone who can," or "It will hold back my advancement" . . . These are typical reasons for denying the existence of Belief-1 problems. The party is the corporate culture that does not permit employees to talk openly about Belief-1 problems. A high-level executive in one of the largest corporations in the world confessed in a 1991 interview that he was "over his head" in his new position. "I can't do it," he said. Yet, he could not bring himself to express this to anyone for fear that the organization would not want to hear it. Neither employee nor employer are well served in situations like this.

The irony in the cover-up of Belief-1 problems is that they tend to be relatively easy to remedy . . . easy compared to the problems they can cause. Like a small nick on the arm that goes untreated, Belief-1 problems can fester into debilitating afflictions of the first order. Look for the "B-1 nicks" in your workforce and treat the problems early so they don't get out of hand. "You can do it."

Clear up Belief-1 problems and the way is opened for motivation to wield its power on performance; allow the problems to fester and motivation never gets out of the blocks.

The Second Belief
"Will Outcomes Be Tied To My Performance?"

The second belief (Belief-2) deals with the relationship between *performance* and *outcomes*. Employees must believe that performing as asked will, indeed, lead to the outcomes offered.

Suppose an employee is offered an *outcome* that will lead to a high level of satisfaction. Further suppose the employee believes "I can do it," but concludes, "My manager always promises things and never delivers. I don't believe I will get the outcome even if I perform well." What happens to the employee's motivation? Needless to say, it suffers. Even when employees are offered what they want, and believe they can do the job (Belief-1), they are not motivated if they believe "Outcomes will not be tied to my performance" (Belief-2).

BELIEF-2
"Will outcomes be tied to my performance?"

Effort ⟶ Performance ⟶ (B-2) Outcomes ⟶ Satisfaction

*"Outcomes will be tied
to my performance."*

*"Outcomes will not be tied
to my performance."*

Belief-2 problems are also widespread in the workplace. The reasons are several:

- It is not always easy to tie outcomes to performance.
- In many instances, performance is difficult to measure.
- There are not always desirable outcomes to give for performance, particularly in hard times.
- Sometimes people possess an inflated sense of their own worth and outcomes seem to be unbefitting the performance delivered.
- Sometimes people misconstrue and expect outcomes based on *effort* rather than *performance*. Effort does not earn outcomes, performance earns outcomes.

Unlike Belief-1, Belief-2 problems are openly discussed by employees, at least among themselves. Unfortunately, expressions of Belief-2 problems are often interpreted by management as something else: complaining. "My performance evaluation was not fair . . . The system of rewards around here stinks . . . You don't get what you deserve here no matter how well you perform" . . . To construe as mere grumbling off-hand comments like these may be to miss a deeper meaning—"Outcomes are not tied to performance." If that is believed, motivation and performance are at risk.

Belief-2 problems are serious business and take a

long time to correct. Fail to deliver on an earned performance bonus given once a year and it's another year before the slight can be corrected; miss again because of an off year in corporate earnings, and a pattern is established in the employee's mind that will take at least a couple of years of "doing as promised" to overcome.

The Third Belief
"Will Outcomes Be Satisfying To Me?"

The third belief (Belief-3) deals with the relationship between *outcomes* and *satisfaction*. This is the classical notion that offering outcomes deemed to be satisfying will produce motivation in-and-of-itself.

Suppose a person believes, "I can do the job and I will get the outcomes if I do," but realizes that the outcomes would not be satisfying. What happens to the motivation of this person? No doubt, it suffers. When people believe that they can do the job (Belief-1) and that outcomes are tied to performance (Belief-2), they are not motivated if they believe the outcomes will be *dissatisfying* (Belief-3). It doesn't make sense for anyone to work hard for something they don't want.

BELIEF-3

"Will outcomes be satisfying to me?"

Effort ⟶ Performance ⟶ Outcomes ⟶(B-3)⟶ Satisfaction

> *"Outcomes will be satisfying to me."*
>
> *"Outcomes will not be satisfying to me."*

Belief-3 problems are a common occurrence in the workplace. Why?

- Managers offer outcomes that are satisfying to themselves in the belief that employees will want the same thing.

- Everyone is offered the same outcome when different things motivate different people. A bass boat is not an attractive outcome for the performance of a person who wants a bigger paycheck; a raise means little to one motivated by recognition or authority . . . .

- The "big-three" outcomes—money, advancement and job security—are assumed to negate the need for praise, recognition, openness, honesty and other important motivating outcomes.

Employees don't so much hide Belief-3 problems as they are vague about them. Employees will let it be known that they are dissatisfied, but may be reluctant to be specific. There's good reason: they know exactly what is causing *their* dissatisfaction, they know what would be more satisfying than the spurned offering, but they need to be *asked*. It is not the kind of unsolicited information that people are normally comfortable volunteering to their boss, who, after all, had some hand in establishing the rejected reward to begin with. Employees are willing to talk about these things if management asks, we have learned over the years. Most managers just never ask, and Belief-3 problems gnaw away at organization after organization. The lost performance can only be guessed at, but the guess is staggering.

The record shows that the Belief System can help restore some of this performance.

The Bottom Line

It is not what is offered but what is believed that counts in the serious business of employee motivation. Certainly, people must be offered what they want, as the popular theories of motivation stress; but, alone, the *offering* is not enough. Employees must believe—in the three ways defined —that they will actually get what is being offered. The motivation to perform occurs *only* when they believe—three ways—that they will, indeed, get what they want. That is the bottom line. Employees are not motivated when managers focus on the *offering* and ignore the *believing*.

In the Belief System approach to motivation, three conditions must exist for people to be motivated.

They must believe, "I can do the job." They must believe, "I will get the outcomes if I perform well." And they must believe, "The outcomes will be satisfying." A deficiency in any one of the three will result in a deficiency in a person's motivation.

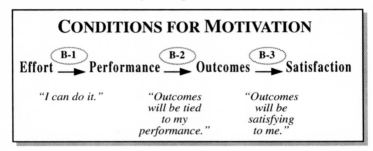

CHAPTER 2

What's The Problem?

When the office computer crashes or the elevator lurches to a stop *between* floors 16 and 17, you are instantly notified of a problem. Not so with motivation. The problem may have been building for some time and be deeply entrenched before it becomes obvious to many busy managers. Indeed, the first step in solving motivation problems is recognizing *when* there is a problem. It is not so difficult to do, but management often does not take the time to read the signs—lack of effort, poor performance, job dissatisfaction, tardiness, absenteeism, missed deadlines and other rather obvious indications that something is wrong. These indicators are not the problem, they are *symptoms* of the problem.

C H A P T E R   2

Symptoms tell us *when* something is wrong but, unfortunately, they don't tell us *what* is wrong. That's the next step—identifying the problem. As easy as that may seem, experience has taught us that identifying motivation problems is anything but easy. The key is knowing what to look for.

The Belief System helps take the guesswork, false starts and missed opportunities out of the search for motivation problems. Specifically, the system alerts management to one or more of the three basic types of employee motivation problems: *lack of confidence*, a Belief-1 (B-1) problem ("I can't do it, I can't meet the performance expectations."); *lack of trust*, a Belief-2 (B-2) problem ("Outcomes will not be tied to my performance."); and *lack of satisfaction*, a Belief-3 (B-3) problem ("The outcomes offered will not be satisfying to me.").

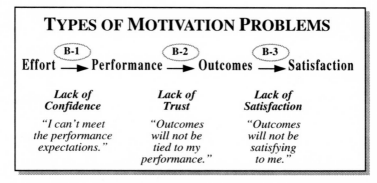

TYPES OF MOTIVATION PROBLEMS

Effort →(B-1)→ Performance →(B-2)→ Outcomes →(B-3)→ Satisfaction

Lack of Confidence	*Lack of Trust*	*Lack of Satisfaction*
"I can't meet the performance expectations."	*"Outcomes will not be tied to my performance."*	*"Outcomes will not be satisfying to me."*

Many managers who use the Belief System are surprised to learn how many of their employees have a *confidence problem* (B-1). "I did not realize how many of my people were not motivated because they didn't believe they could do what was expected," noted one senior executive of a large service company. "In some cases they weren't clear about what to do; others simply were not sure how to get it done. My mistake was I *assumed* they could do it. I thought because they were bright, hard working and had similar work experiences they would naturally be motivated. I was wrong."

The *trust problem* (B-2) is particularly widespread in corporate America today. Repeatedly, we see managers telling employees that if they do well they will be rewarded, but the rewards rarely come. Whatever the reasons for this, it is our experience that these promises become hollow to employees and a general lack of trust develops. This is a quick way to destroy an organization.

Another twist on the trust problem (B-2) is readily apparent in public reaction to media reports about the earnings of senior executives in major corporations. Survey after survey shows that employees don't think the disparity in income levels between "them and us" is justified. "Performance does not warrant the outcomes (B-2) enjoyed by senior executives," is the message.

The prevalence of *satisfaction problems* (B-3) comes as a surprise to many first-time users of the Belief System. It is no surprise to us. We see it frequently in the best and the worst of organizations.

One manager recently trained in the use of the Belief System made the point with this observation, "Once I started focusing on the individuality of my employees, I was shocked to find how diverse they are in terms of what motivates them. I had been working hard to treat everyone the same. As a result, I had created a lot of dissatisfaction for everybody. Assuming the same incentives would have the same impact on everyone was a huge mistake. I really felt foolish when I realized I was causing so much dissatisfaction. I'd been doing this for years. 'Makes you wonder how many other managers out there are making the same mistake."

Getting To The Problem

So now you know what to look for: a B-1, B-2 or B-3 problem, but *how* do you find them? Keeping your eyes open is not enough. You can't be everywhere and see everything.

There is one best answer to the question of how to identify motivation problems—go to the source, the one with the problem, the employee. Simply put, *if you want to know what the problem is, ask.* After more than 50 years of combined experience in working with managers, we remain intrigued by the unwillingness of management to simply ask employees what's behind rather conspicuous motivation problems. Perhaps some of the answer lies in this response from the general manager of a large TV station: "I don't ask because I'm afraid I'll find out! And then I'll have to deal with it."

Most people are glad to tell you what the problem is, especially when they believe you want to help. All you have to do is get the answers to a few thoughtful questions.

Questions To Be Answered

Managers must look for the *answers* to three core questions, each one a derivation of the B-1, B-2 or B-3 problem. How the questions are posed or worded can vary, as noted below, but the objective remains the same—what are the answers to these questions?

- *Does the person believe his or her effort will lead to the expected performance? (B-1)*
- *Does the person believe the outcomes will be tied to his or her performance? (B-2)*
- *Does the person believe the outcomes will be satisfying? (B-3)*

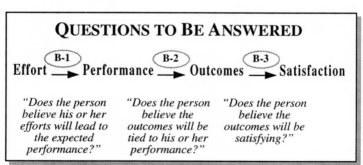

QUESTIONS TO BE ANSWERED

Effort $\xrightarrow{\text{B-1}}$ Performance $\xrightarrow{\text{B-2}}$ Outcomes $\xrightarrow{\text{B-3}}$ Satisfaction

| *"Does the person believe his or her efforts will lead to the expected performance?"* | *"Does the person believe the outcomes will be tied to his or her performance?"* | *"Does the person believe the outcomes will be satisfying?"* |

C H A P T E R   2

Questions To Ask

"Ask not for a 'deal' when its steak you want for its entrails and tripe I will give you," said the butcher to a haggling patron. Getting the right answer is a product of asking the right question. It's true in the meat business, true in the Belief System, true where ever truth is sought. Here are some questions that get to the truth of the matter with motivation and performance problems.

For answers to the Belief-1 question, managers might ask:

- *"Do you know what is expected?"*
- *"Do you think what's expected is attainable?"*
- *"Can you do what is being asked of you?"*
- *"Can you finish the work on time?"*
- *"Do you see any problem in doing what you are being asked to do?"*

Answers to Belief-2 questions can come from questions like these:

- *"What is being offered for good performance?"*
- *"In your opinion, have we come through on our promises in the past?"*
- *"Do you expect to get what is being offered?"*
- *"What do you expect to get if you do a good job?"*
- *"What do you expect to happen if you perform poorly?"*

To find answers to the Belief-3 question, these questions work well:

- *"What would be satisfying to you?"*
- *"Is the work meaningful to you?"*
- *"Is there anything you don't want?"*
- *"Do you want the things being offered?"*
- *"Do you want something that is not being offered?"*

Responses to Expect

What might an attentive manager hear in response to the preceding questions? It depends on whether or not there are motivation problems at work in the ranks. Consider:

For any of the Belief-1 questions, a confident person might respond by saying, "No problem. That's a piece of cake." Clearly, the person is saying, "I can do it." Belief-1, a lack of confidence, does not appear to be a problem. But the answer may well be different—"You've got to be kidding. I can't do that, no way." Here, there is a problem, a Belief-1 *lack of confidence* problem. "I can't do it" comes through loud and clear. Responses won't always be so demonstrative and unmistakable, but the truth will be clear enough to the careful listener. And it is in the managers best interest to listen well and to ferret out the truth. People who believe that they cannot meet performance expectations are hamstrung and so is the organization that employs them. The confidence problem may easily be solved but until it is, motivation and performance suffer.

To the Belief-2 questions, people may respond in this way, "You can count on what's said here. Produce and you'll be well rewarded; sluff off and you're out the door." These are people who believe that "Outcomes are tied to performance." No reason to believe that a Belief-2 problem, lack of trust, exists in such cases. To the same questions, respondents might also say, "Work hard, work smart or lay on your butt and talk the day away—it's all the same here. Nobody seems to care." What is expressed is plain, "Outcomes are not tied to performance." A Belief-2 *trust problem* is at work. Believing that outcomes will not be tied to performance holds people back and dampens motivation and performance. It is not a problem to be taken lightly.

Belief-3 questions could yield a response along these lines—"You do that for me and I'll give this company my first-borne child." Would you guess this employee to believe that the "Outcomes will be satisfying?" No reason to believe otherwise. But not so with this—"That's no reward for me, I don't want more responsibility." No guesswork in this instance—"The outcome will not be satisfying." A Belief-3 *lack of satisfaction* problem is indicated. It can weigh as heavily on employee motivation and performance as the other two problems.

Strange things happen when employees begin

earnestly to respond to the kinds of questions prescribed here. Managers who do not have the high ground of the Belief System from which to see could easily interpret the feedback as complaints and the respondents as complainers. A litany of negative consequences could result. Valuable employees . . . may be labeled as complainers. What they say or do from then on may be discounted. They may be avoided thereafter (managers don't like to be around complainers any more than anyone else). Less communication with these employees could occur in the future. The employees could be expected to get upset with the "distancing" of their manager. Relations between employees and manager would surely deteriorate. Job satisfaction for both parties would go down. And so on, and so on . . . .

But managers operating under the tenants of the Belief System see things differently. Employee feedback, openly and honestly solicited and forthrightly given, is seen for what it is: an unparalleled opportunity to set things right in the workforce. Comments that previously would have been viewed as a bad attitude, resistance or insubordination are viewed instead as valuable information, the vital ingredient in a plan of action that can correct motivation and performance problems before they drag down an organization. For these managers, it is not complaining for an employee to say, "You never get what you deserve around here," or "I don't like that part of my job"; there is no reason to doubt the capabilities of a person who says, "I don't know if I can do that or not."

With these kinds of answers, employees are indicating problems on the job and they are asking for help in solving them. Seen this way, managers:

- Listen carefully.
- Ask more questions to better understand.
- Determine what is wrong.
- Seek the employee's solutions.
- Thank the employees for bringing the situation to their attention.
- Fix the problems.
- Watch happy employees work harder and perform better.

Responses In Combination

Sometimes the identity of a motivation problem is easier to determine when the results of B-2 and B-3 questioning are combined. For example, if a person says, "I will get the outcome if I perform well (B-2), and it is something I want" (B-3), there is *not* a motivation problem. On the other hand, the following combination of responses indicates a problem—"I will get the outcome if I perform well (B-2), but it is something I *don't* want" (B-3). There is a satisfaction (B-3) problem at work here. When a person thinks, "I will not get the outcome even if I perform well (B-2), but it is not something I want anyway" (B-3), there is *not* a problem. There is a problem, however when someone believes—"I do not believe I will get the outcome even if I perform well (B-2), and it is something I want" (B-3). A trust (B-2) problem is the culprit.

In other words, when a person believes *either* that performance will lead to outcomes that are not wanted *or* that performance will not lead to outcomes that are wanted, there is little motivation to expend the effort necessary to perform well.

IDENTIFYING MOTIVATION PROBLEMS BY COMBINING BELIEF-2 AND BELIEF-3

Effort ⟶ Performance ⟶ Outcomes ⟶ Satisfaction

1. *"I will get the outcome if I perform well (Belief-2), and it is something I want" (Belief-3). This is not a problem.*

2. *"I will get the outcome if I perform well (Belief-2), but it is something I don't want" (Belief-3). This is a problem – a Belief-3 problem.*

3. *"I will not get the outcome if I perform well (Belief-2), but it is something I don't want" (Belief-3). This is not a problem.*

4. *"I will not get the outcome if I perform well (Belief-2), and it is something I want" (Belief-3). This is a problem – a Belief-2 problem.*

Interpreting The Responses

Once a middle-aged father and corporate executive asked his teenage daughter for an opinion on a young man she knew. "Oh, he's bad, Dad; I mean, we're talking bad!" whereupon the no-nonsense father struck the young man's name from the company's summer intern roll. Despite the chagrined daughter's subsequent protestations that bad isn't bad, but *good,* there was no job to be had that summer for the bad (good) young man. The point? Make sure that what you hear is the message that is being conveyed. Remember, you, the manager, are trying to identify motivation and performance problems. Asking the right questions is crucial, but misinterpretation of the answers will get you off in the wrong direction and doom your efforts.

Experience has taught us that the best way to avoid "missing the point" is to log employee responses into a simple rating scale. Precision is not a factor in this scale. Thoughtful "guesstimates" work just fine. If you can, with some confidence, generally rate a person's beliefs (B-1, B-2, B-3), there is good reason to believe that you have learned what the person really believes. If you cannot with reasonable confidence so rate the person's beliefs, you need more information. Using the rating scale helps you to *know what you know.*

The Belief-1 rating scale has a range of zero to ten. Zero represents the negative variation of the belief "I *cannot* perform as expected." A rating of ten represents the positive expression, "I *can* perform as expected."

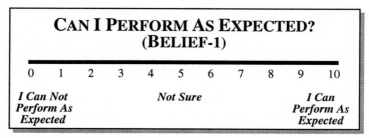

A similar scale is used for Belief-2. The "I will *not* get outcomes based on my performance" belief is represented by a zero; the other end of the scale, a ten, is the positive, "I will *get* outcomes based on performance."

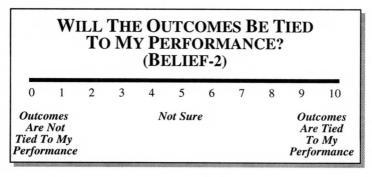

C H A P T E R   2

The Belief-3 rating scale differs from the previous two. It reflects the degree of satisfaction *or* dissatisfaction with an outcome or combination of outcomes. The B-3 scale ranges from -10, the highest *dissatisfaction* rating, to +10, the highest *satisfaction* rating.

WILL THE OUTCOMES BE SATISFYING TO ME? (BELIEF-3)

-10	-8	-6	-4	-2	0	+2	+4	+6	+8	+10

Outcomes Very Dissatisfying	*Outcomes Slightly Dissatisfying*	*Outcomes Slightly Satisfying*	*Outcomes Very Satisfying*

Here, then, is how a manager might interpret Belief-1, Belief-2, and Belief-3 comments from employees.

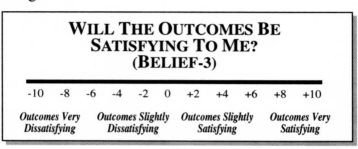

INTERPRETING BELIEF-1 STATEMENTS

0	1	2	3	4	5	6	7	8	9	10

I Can Not Perform As Expected	*Not Sure*	*I Can Perform As Expected*
• *"I can't do it."*	• *"I'm not sure I can do it."*	• *"I can do it."*
• *"There is no way."*	• *"I might be able to."*	• *"No problem."*
• *"It's impossible."*	• *"Maybe I can do it."*	• *"That's easy."*
• *"I don't know how."*	• *"The odds are even."*	• *"No sweat."*
• *"I haven't any idea what's expected of me."*	• *"I'm not sure what's expected of me."*	• *"I know exactly what's expected of me."*

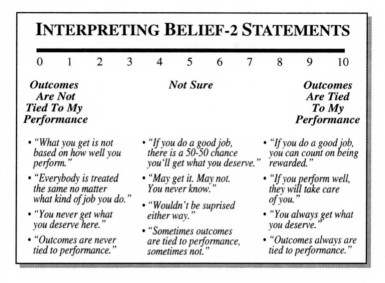

INTERPRETING BELIEF-2 STATEMENTS

0	1	2	3	4	5	6	7	8	9	10

Outcomes Are Not Tied To My Performance — *Not Sure* — *Outcomes Are Tied To My Performance*

- *"What you get is not based on how well you perform."*
- *"Everybody is treated the same no matter what kind of job you do."*
- *"You never get what you deserve here."*
- *"Outcomes are never tied to performance."*

- *"If you do a good job, there is a 50-50 chance you'll get what you deserve."*
- *"May get it. May not. You never know."*
- *"Wouldn't be suprised either way."*
- *"Sometimes outcomes are tied to performance, sometimes not."*

- *"If you do a good job, you can count on being rewarded."*
- *"If you perform well, they will take care of you."*
- *"You always get what you deserve."*
- *"Outcomes always are tied to performance."*

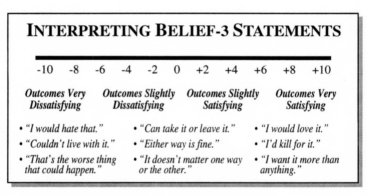

INTERPRETING BELIEF-3 STATEMENTS

-10	-8	-6	-4	-2	0	+2	+4	+6	+8	+10

Outcomes Very Dissatisfying — *Outcomes Slightly Dissatisfying* — *Outcomes Slightly Satisfying* — *Outcomes Very Satisfying*

- *"I would hate that."*
- *"Couldn't live with it."*
- *"That's the worse thing that could happen."*

- *"Can take it or leave it."*
- *"Either way is fine."*
- *"It doesn't matter one way or the other."*

- *"I would love it."*
- *"I'd kill for it."*
- *"I want it more than anything."*

O.K., you have completed your ratings, now what are you looking at? How are you assisted in sorting out motivation problems? The first step is to apply the following rules of thumb to the scale.

Rule of Thumb #1	If the rating is on the upper third of the rating scale, there is *no* reason to suspect a problem.
Rule of Thumb #2	If a rating is in the middle third of the scale, there is a *potential* problem.
Rule of Thumb #3	If a rating is in the lower third of the scale, there *definitely* is a problem.

Next thing is to apply a little deductive reasoning. Let's suppose you interviewed a job applicant employing the Belief System of questioning and the B-1, B-2 and B-3 rating scales. After a careful interview process, you conclude that the person's beliefs about the job available would be accurately stated by assigning a rating of "5" to Belief-1, a "9" to Belief-2 and a "+8" to Belief-3. The proper interpretation is that the person is not particularly confident about being able to do the job (Belief-1 = 5). There is a potential motivation and performance problem here. The applicant is nearly certain of "getting the outcomes" if performance is good (Belief-2 = 9), and believes the "outcomes will be satisfying" (Belief-3 = +8). Based on this, you would not expect this person to have a Belief-2 or Belief-3 motivation problem.

How about a top performer whose work has fallen off recently? After talking with this person and asking a few questions, you rate him at 9, 10, and -8 for Beliefs 1, 2, and 3, respectively. What do you conclude? The person believes "I can perform as expected" (Belief-1 = 9), so there is not a Belief-1 problem. The person is certain outcomes will be based on performance (Belief-2 = 10), but the outcomes are viewed as very dissatisfying (Belief-3 = -8). You have a motivation problem, and you know what it is!

It may be that you have gathered all the information necessary to recognize a problem but you still don't see it; the information is in hand, *you just don't know you have it.* Rating an employee's "three beliefs" is an excellent device for forcing managers to see whether they have learned all that they need to know. Furthermore, the rating scales bring out the full meaning of what you have learned. For example, a manager we know noticed that a new employee was having a little trouble catching on to some technical requirements of his job. The problem was not unusual and the manager, busy out of the office, gave it no further thought. A couple weeks later, the employee expressed dissatisfaction with how things were going with the job. Nothing else was said and there were no other signs of a problem for a time. Then the person mentioned to the manager that he was upset about the company's across-the-board pay raise policy.

Three isolated incidents, right? Wrong. Put it all on the rating scales, and you see a different picture. The employee's Belief-1 is probably not high, though you don't know enough to rate it. Belief-2 for pay is low—he thought he should have earned more than the across-the-board raise. Belief-3 is negative, again for reasons that are not exactly clear. This information viewed in isolation does not suggest anything particularly troublesome, but when observed together it is clear that the employee is not motivated nearly as much as he or she could be. This person is experiencing each of the three belief problems.

Summary

With the Belief System, the process for identifying motivation problems begins with the recognition of symptoms. A decline in performance or the beginning of an undesirable behavior, are examples. When symptoms are noticed, it is important to immediately start determining what the problem is. The primary means for doing this is talking with the person.

There are three questions to be answered:
- *Does the person believe his or her effort will lead to the expected performance? (Belief-1)*
- *Does the person believe the outcomes will be tied to his or her performance? (Belief-2)*
- *Does the person believe the outcomes will be satisfying? (Belief-3)*

WHAT'S THE PROBLEM?

All three beliefs must be relatively strong for a person to be motivated. If they are not, you have identified a motivation problem.

There is considerable latitude in the questions you can ask to determine the three beliefs. Interpreting responses to the questions is made easier with a rating scale. Beliefs that fall in the middle third of the rating scales suggest potential problems, while ratings in the lower third indicate definite motivation problems.

Remember, the bottom line is this: in order to be motivated, people must have *confidence in themselves* to meet performance expectations, *trust in others* to tie outcomes to performance, and be *satisfied with the outcomes* they are to receive.

CHAPTER 3

Causes and
Solutions

Sitting face-to-face with her boss, discouraged, and uncomfortable, she confessed, "I have no experience with this kind of work. I don't know if I can do it." He recognized the problem right away and knew exactly what to do. All she needed was some encouragement. A good pep talk would do the trick. Four weeks later she resigned, leaving behind a project that never got off the ground.

One of the most common mistakes in handling motivation and performance problems is identifying the *problem*, then jumping ahead to *solutions* without first determining the *causes* of the problem. This is a hit-or-miss proposition with poor odds for success. It can cause more problems than it solves.

Uncovering Causes

When she said, "I have no experience with this kind of work," she wasn't looking for a pep talk. She knew what was *causing* the problem and how to solve it. All she wanted was someone to listen. All she needed was a little help to make her solution work. When her manager quickly jumped ahead to *his* solution, as he usually did, she decided it was hopeless.

The situation would likely have been far different had the manager responded, "Why do you think you can't pull it off?" It is important for managers to focus first on what is *causing* the problem, rather than jumping ahead to solutions.

Effective communication is the key to identifying the causes of motivation problems. In the Belief System that means going to the source, *ask the employee*. Here's why. First, employees generally are willing to talk when they have a problem. Second, and perhaps most important, the person with the problem is undoubtedly the best source of information about what is causing it.

Asking can take many forms, some that are effective, some that lead to less than candid answers and employee distrust. It's important that the questions be open, neutral and probing; you want the truth, the facts, so that sound decisions can be made. Be careful, therefore, to *avoid leading questions*. They beget answers employees think managers want to hear, not the ones on their minds or in their hearts. These examples get the point across: "You don't think the problem is really *that* serious, do you?" Or, "Now that the plant manager is gone, we won't have that problem again, will we?"

Here are some simple questions of the open, neutral and probing kind that have proven effective:

- Why do you feel that way?
- Can you tell me more?
- What is behind your thinking on this?
- What happened to make you feel that way?
- Can you tell me what is going on?
- Can you be more specific?

Each of these questions, and many others like them, give people the opportunity and encouragement they need to talk. *Asking* is the way to uncover the *causes* of motivation problems. As simple and self-evident as that seems, the facts are that managers generally don't ask. There are managers who have an inflated opinion of themselves (they think they know it all, and don't need to ask the opinion of others). Some managers are bound by tradition, "I'm the guy in charge here, *I'm* suppose to decide these things . . . ." Afraid that they will have to deal with unpleasant issues, many managers prefer not to ask. There is the fear in a few managers that their incompetence will be exposed if they get into face-to-face question-and-answer sessions with employees . . . . These are but a few of the reasons. Clearing away such obstacles to effective manager-employee communications is one of the single most valuable benefits garnered from the Belief System.

What Will You Find?

When you probe for the *causes* of motivation problems, what can you expect to find? It depends. The causes are different for each of the three types of motivation problems described in this and the previous chapter—*lack of confidence* (Belief-1), *lack of trust* (Belief-2), and *lack of satisfaction* (Belief-3). Let's take a look at the causes of each.

Causes of Confidence Problems

What are the primary causes of confidence (Belief-1) problems? What causes people to say, "I can't do it, I can't perform as expected?"

Inadequate Skills—When employees do not have adequate skills for the job they are expected to perform it should not be surprising that they might conclude, "I can't do it." It is a common refrain in our business. Organizations give employees considerable responsibility, but they don't always prepare them for it. It is not a situation to breed confidence. We have found motivation suffers and effort and performance decline. Particularly vulnerable to this problem are employees in work arrangements that are relatively self-managed and independent. Without the attendant skills for the job at hand, individual and group confidence sags and things bog down.

Unrealistic Expectations— Organizations that stress performance, quality, and profitability often set standards so high that the stretch required of employees to meet them becomes a negative, and employees conclude, "I can't do it." This is particularly common during economic downturns and downsizing. Fewer and fewer employees are called on to carry heavier and heavier workloads. The pressure to survive causes organizations to impose unrealistic expectations on the workforce. When employees start saying, "this is impossible," they tend to give up.

Unclear Expectations— When people are not sure what is expected, they commence to have doubts about their ability to get the job done. The CEO who fails to give his direct-reports proper guidance, for example, creates uncertainty about what is expected. Quite predictably, these people will begin to question themselves. Enthusiasm will wane, followed by a fall in performance. It can really set a company back.

There are other causes of *confidence (B-1) problems* that need to find a permanent place in management's consciousness.

- People with a *history of failure* tend to give up, and say, "I can't do it." This is a surprisingly complex issue that works to the detriment of a shocking number of employees. The pattern of failure can develop as a child and carry over into the workplace or it can spring from a single traumatic mistake or setback; it can manifest itself as subtle nagging doubts about one's ability to do certain things (reducing B-1 levels accordingly) or it can be a virtual brick wall (zero B-1) to one's value as an employee in specific situations.

- *Inadequate resources or authority* can impact confidence (B-1). You can't cross a 10-foot crevasse on an 8-foot board, and you can't do the job the boss wants if the resources needed to do it are not available. The only surprise in this situation is that so many managers are surprised to learn that their employees have no confidence in their ability to do the job. Resources imply many things: facilities, equipment, personnel, information, finances . . . and *authority*. Having all the tools at hand to do the job won't get it done if the person responsible for the work doesn't have the authority to put things in motion. Expect debilitating confidence (B-1) problems without it.

- Flaws and quirks in one's *management style* can be a painful contributor to employee confidence (B-1) problems. Project a tough perfectionist reputation with employees and watch confidence sag as one after another concludes, "I can't measure up, I can't do it." The same results follow harsh criticism of poor performance, failure to acknowledge good performance, a poor match of job requirements and employee skills and not enough structure in a job ("I'm not sure what you want from me? I don't know if I can do it or not . . . ."). Digging out of your own managerial shortcomings is not easy. It's hard to be objective, to see yourself as others do; but it's imperative if your employees are adversely effected by your manner.

• *Organizational factors* play a big role in employee confidence. All things equal, a well-trained employee is confident, one who is not is not. Is the company's rapid growth pushing employees beyond their training and resources? If so, a Belief System manager will see it reflected in B-1 problems. Rapid technological changes are a certain source of confidence problems if skills are not diligently updated. Hiring people with the wrong qualifications for the job will produce employees with low B-1 levels. Under-staffing will overload personnel, put them behind and dampen confidence in getting the job done. High employee turnover usually means less qualified (less confident) people replace higher qualified (more confident) people, and well qualified (and confident) employees find themselves in tandem with increasingly less qualified (and less confident) associates, diminishing the former's belief that the work will get done correctly and on time. The overall result is the emergence of a wholesale belief that, "I (we) can't do it."

Causes of Trust Problems

There are several primary causes of trust (Belief-2) problems, i.e., "What I get is not based on my performance."

Outcomes Are Not Tied To Performance— Some organizations simply do not have systems in place that reward people based on performance. Others promise to link rewards to performance, but don't follow through. The practice of "promising and not delivering" can have serious impact on a company, as we previously noted.

Whether it is the absence of reward systems, or systems that do not work, the end result is the same. High performers go unrewarded and poor performers are not penalized. The high performers ask, "Why should I do a good job when it doesn't pay off?" Poor performers say, "Why should I work harder?"

Differences In Perceptions— It is not unusual for managers and employees to define performance differently. "Results" most often is the manager's definition—increased production, improved quality, reduced costs and higher profit. Employees can come to believe that performance means coming to work every day, being on time, having a good attitude and working hard. While these traits may lead to the kind of results managers look for, they are not the same as results. Effort does not equal performance. Trying is not the same as getting the job done. When managers and employees define performance differently, expect trust (B-2) problems to occur. An employee who is never absent, who puts in an honest days work and keeps his nose clean expects to be rewarded for it. When the manager, who is looking for results, does not reward the employee, he feels cheated. "I didn't get what I deserved," is the conclusion, or "outcomes are not tied to performance." This is a common problem. Even when outcomes are tied closely to performance, employees may perceive they are not. The *misperception* causes a downturn in employee motivation with predictable effects on effort and performance.

A History Of Outcomes Not Being Tied To Performance— Employees who have a history of not getting what they deserve tend to hold well-entrenched beliefs that outcomes are not tied to performance. Bureaucracies, corporate and otherwise, often feel the bite of this problem. Outcomes must be tied closely to performance *over a long period* for people to change long-held beliefs that have been reinforced for years.

Causes of Satisfaction Problems

What are the primary causes of satisfaction (Belief- 3) problems? What causes employees to say, "The outcomes are not satisfying to me?" There are two main causes.

Not Receiving Desired Outcomes— Satisfaction problems often arise simply because employees are not getting what they want. It is not always the big or obvious things that are desired—more money, a big promotion or improved job security. No serious student of human motivation fails to recognize the importance of "little things" in prompting employees to extend themselves, little things like getting treated with more respect, getting more responsibility, getting management's attentive ear when there is a problem. To fail to extend these offerings as legitimate and coveted rewards for performance is to carry "half a quiver" into the hunt for managerial excellence. Don't forget: any time employees want something that they are not getting (B-3), motivation and performance are the losers.

Receiving Unwanted Outcomes— The second major cause of B-3 problems is as basic as the first. Employees often are given outcomes they do not want. Not all people desire additional responsibility, greater empowerment or more overtime, for example. When people receive undesired outcomes for their performance, there should be no surprise to find that they are not as satisfied as they might be. Motivation, in this instance, cannot be expected to flourish.

With these causes in mind, think about this . . . young people today look for different things in a job than previous generations; the justification (if there ever was one) for treating everyone the same is gone. Treat all employees alike today and you run the substantial risk of *simultaneously* denying them what they want, and giving them things they don't want. That is a sure formula for trouble.

There are other causes of *satisfaction (B-3) problems* that should not escape the scrutiny of management. The problem arises when employees *under-value* outcomes received and *over-value* outcomes not received; and it occurs when people are confused about what they want, are undergoing preference changes and experiencing conflicting desires. Let's examine each more closely.

- *Under-valuing outcomes received*—There is a manager we know who valued a young MBA so much that he put the youngster in a seemingly obscure assignment for the company's crusty manufacturing VP. A top performance, the manager knew, would put the MBA on a fast track up the corporate ladder. Concurrent with this assignment, however, the manager offered a less strategic promotion to another employee. You can imagine the manager's surprise when his pet project floundered with B-3 problems—the MBA wanted the promotion he didn't get, and did not see the value in the assignment he did get.

- *Over-valuing outcomes not received*—In a balancing act to keep two valued employees happy with but one spot to fill on a key advisory committee, the manager gave the loser a reserved parking space near the branch office doorway. Unbeknownst to the manager, the winner of the committee seat coveted the parking space far beyond its value in the total scheme of things, and his B-3 motivation level actually fell.

- *Confusion over what is wanted*—How about the person who is offered a new "territory" that will pay more money and move him closer to the seat of corporate power, but will require relocation and mean more pressure to perform? The potential satisfaction of more money and better exposure is very attractive, but the relocation and added pressure are not. What to do? The person doesn't know. He can't make up his mind. His values are confused; dissatisfaction seems eminent whatever the decision. Confused values can cause frequent, even dramatic shifts in employee satisfaction (B-3) levels.

- *Preference changes*—Then there is the case of the happy, hardworking, productive employee who, after a settling marriage, loses enthusiasm for his travel-heavy job. Simply put, the value he once placed on frequent excursions to San Francisco, Hong Kong and Singapore gave way to a desire to be home more with his wife. From a high "+9" or "+10" on the job satisfaction (B-3) rating scale to a negative "-3" or "-4", and nothing changed but a marital status . . . Unusual? Certainly not. Changed values are a major source of satisfaction (B-3) problems in the workplace.

• *Conflicting desires*—The manager of the newlywed just introduced went to work accommodating his employee's under-standable desire to "get off the road" and spend more time with his new wife. The job the manager found seemed to fill the bill— same money, open-ended advancement possibilities, 9-to-5 hours with nothing more than an annual convention to take him out of town. There was just one snag—he had a sinking feeling that he wouldn't like the work. "I've done that kind of thing before," he explained, "and it's just not something I much enjoy. I don't know what to do." He was caught in a conflict of desires. "Enjoying the job" had long been a motivating factor in his life. Now he was faced with doing work he didn't like because his values had changed.

The conflicting desires played havoc on his satisfaction (B-3) level.

* *Work itself is not rewarding—* Some employees like their jobs; others don't. When the work itself is not rewarding, a satisfaction problem (B-3) is sure to exist.

Solution Approaches Are Obvious

When the *causes* of motivation problems are identified, *general solutions* to the problems become self-evident. A confidence (B-1) problem caused by an employee's unfamiliarity with a new computer system, for example, points directly to some sort of training program to overcome the deficiency and eliminate the problem. You wouldn't know this if you didn't know the *cause* of the problem. (The specifics of the solution, which we will explain later, are developed in a collaborative effort between manager and employee.) Learning the causes of motivation problems also "de-mystifies" the approaches taken to solve them. We have learned from considerable experience that proceeding directly from the identification of a *problem* to its *solution* without first determining the causes creates an element of uncertainty or mystery that can be unsettling. Solution approaches suffer in an air of uncertainty. The mystery is removed by proceeding from the *problem*, to the *causes*, then to the *solutions*.

C H A P T E R   3

Causes And Solution Approaches Go Hand-In-Hand

Motivation Problem	Typical Causes	Obvious Solution Approaches
Confidence (Belief-1)	• Inadequate skills	• Provide training, coaching and other forms of skill building; redesign the job; turnover; terminate
	• Unrealistic performance expectations	• Establish realistic expectations, introduce more effective ways to meet expectations, provide more resources
	• Unclear performance expectations	• Establish and/or clarify what is expected
	• History of failure	• Be supportive, create opportunities for success
	• Inadequate resources or authority	•Infuse the resources and authority required of the job
	• Overdemanding management style	• Loosen up, reduce expectations to fit reality, be supportive
	• Growth and change	• Institute or upgrade training regimen
	• Wrong job qualifications	• Reevaluate hiring practices
	• Understaffing	• Reduce workloads or introduce labor/time-saving techniques
	• High employee turnover	• Examine and reduce turnover

Causes And Solution Approaches Go Hand-In-Hand

Motivation Problem	Typical Causes	Obvious Solution Approaches
Trust (Belief-2)	• Outcomes are not tied to performance	• Provide outcomes based on performance
	• Employee and manager define performance differently	• Clarify performance expectations
	• History of outcomes not being tied to performance	• Consistently give outcomes based on performance
Satisfaction (Belief-3)	• Not receiving desired outcomes	• Give desired outcomes when appropriate
	• Receiving unwanted outcomes	• Withhold unwanted outcomes when appropriate
	• Undervaluing outcomes received	• Show where the value lies
	• Overvaluing outcomes not received	• Balance inflated perceptions with the facts, good *and* bad
	• Confusion over what is wanted	• Clarify the situation
	• Preference changes	• Accommodate the changes where possible
	• Conflicting desires	• Make it easier to accommodate the undesirable outcome
	• The work itself is not rewarding	• Redesign the job, transfer, terminate

C H A P T E R 3

The solution approaches referenced thus far are inadequate in certain situations. For example, managers may not have the authority to redesign jobs, organizations may not have reward systems that tie outcomes to performance, and managers may not have the control over outcomes employees want. What can the manager do in these circumstances? This question is addressed extensively in chapter four, "Handling Difficult Problems." But know this about seemingly insoluble motivation problems: managers tend to assume that employees want more than they are actually seeking. In one company we worked with, for example, employees were complaining about not being able to see where to park. Management's response was, "Putting up lights in the parking lot is not feasible." It turned out, with a little Belief System probing into the causes of the dissatisfaction, that all the employees wanted was clear white lines on the asphalt to separate the cars properly. Management, somewhat sheepishly, allowed that, yes, they could take care of the problem afterall.

Effective communication, asking the right questions of the right people, getting to the causes of problems so as to better see their solutions. . . nearly all motivation problems are solvable with the right approach.

Deciding Exactly What To Do

Solution approaches provide *general* guidance in solving motivation problems. They point you in the right direction. That's important, but not enough. What about *specific* solutions? How are they derived?

While causes clearly point the way to solution approaches, *specific* solutions are not self-evident. This is a problem. A big one. And the problem is usually one managers bring upon themselves. You see a motivation problem, identify the cause(s), and the solution approach becomes obvious. *Then the manager tends to feel responsible for developing the specific solution, in all its detail alone.* This is the mistake. Think about it.

What happens when employees have motivation problems? They live with the problem every day. They think about what's wrong and how to fix it. They know the causes. They know the solutions. It isn't a guessing game with them. It's their problem. They know what will fix it. Yes, employees are the best source of information for solutions to motivation problems.

Remember, *if you want to know how to solve a motivation problem, ask the person with the problem.* A simple question can yield handsome returns. Here are some sample questions:

• What is the best way to handle this?

- What do you think we should do?
- Do you have any suggestions?
- How can I help?

Employee solutions will not be acceptable to managers one-hundred percent of the time. Yet, they cannot be ignored. Solutions suggested by employees tend to be less complicated, less costly, and more effective. Getting employees involved in solving their own motivation problems pays off. Because it pays off, and Belief System managers are quick to see it, many go beyond *encouraging* employee involvement in solving motivation and performance problems. These managers see the Belief System process as a *shared responsibility* between manager and employee and go to some pains to instill the thinking in all employees, managers or not.

An Illustration

A group of managers recently completed a training program on the approach to motivation and performance described in this book. Here is a discussion that took place afterwards between one of these managers and an employee.

Employee:

"You have always been pleased with my work, but now that my job has been expanded, I'm not sure I can handle it." (Sounds like a Belief-1 problem—"I can't do it.")

The temptation for the manager was to lapse into a pep talk, something like, "Sure you can. It'll just take a little time. I can let somebody help you for a while until you get things under control." However, this would be jumping ahead to a solution without identifying the causes. The manager had a more appropriate response.

Manager:
> "You have done good work and I have never seen you question your ability to get the job done. Why are you having doubts now?" (If you want to know what is causing a motivation problem, *ask*.)

Employee:
> "There aren't enough hours in the day to get everything done. (Cause—"unrealistic expectations.") And besides that, a couple of my new responsibilities are really technical and I don't have the background to do them." (Cause—"inadequate skills.")

With the causes identified, solutions jumped out. A typical response would be for the manager to say, "It may be hard to change your responsibilities now, but I can get you some training right away." (Solution—"skill building.") This would be offering a solution without considering any ideas the employee may have. Fortunately, the manager resisted the tendency to solve the problem himself and, instead, turned to the employee.

C H A P T E R   3

Manager:

"Do you have a solution in mind?" (If you want to know how to solve a motivation problem, *ask*.)

Employee:

"When we were given new responsibilities, three of us ended up with things we don't feel comfortable doing. Maybe we could change some assignments around? (Solution—"job redesign.") I've talked with the other two. They think it's a good idea."

Manager:

"O.K. I'd like for the three of you to get together and decide exactly what you want to do. Then let's all meet to be sure we are in agreement."

According to the manager, this was not a solution he would have thought about. He had learned that when employees have a problem, they know the causes and they have preferred solutions. While you may not always be able to live with employee suggestions, it pays to ask.

Summary

A common mistake when dealing with motivation problems is to quickly jump ahead to solutions without knowing what is causing the problem. This does not lead to workable solutions.

Motivation problems have specific, identifiable causes. You must find out what they are if you want to solve the problem. The best way to identify causes is to ask.

Solution approaches tend to be self-evident once the causes are identified. Specific solutions are less obvious. If you want to identify good ones, ask.

The person experiencing a motivation problem is the best source of information about causes and solutions. People usually are eager to help solve their own problems. All they need is opportunity and encouragement.

Handling Difficult Problems

The repeated cries of Chicken Little that "the sky is falling" calls for a solution of patience and understanding. But now and then, the sky seems surely to have collapsed, and the solutions get a lot tougher. It's like that with motivation problems. All too frequently, the search for solutions bumps the manager up against problems that have no easy or apparent answers. What do you do about the really difficult problems of motivation and performance? Problems like these, for example:

- An employee wants a promotion, but there are no opportunities available now or in the immediate future.
- An employee wants more money, but the organization is strapped and doesn't have it to give.

- A top performer is not being rewarded fairly and there is little the manager can do about it.
- An employee doesn't like the work and wants to do something different, but other opportunities are not available in the company.
- An employee suffers under pay inequities that cannot be remedied because top management will not permit it, or because the company does not have the resources to do it at present.
- Other employees are responding to the need for higher productivity, while one who has gotten by with marginal work for a long time refuses to change.
- A manager has inherited a low producing, older employee who is trying to hold on for a few more years until retirement.
- An employee simply cannot do the job, and there are no options available in the company or out.

In cases like these, the Belief System manager simply shifts the hunt for solutions into 4-wheel drive; the terrain is tougher, so more torque is put into the climb.

Probe/Check

Before wading into the tall grass of motivation problems, it is a good idea for managers to take stock and make sure they know what they think they know about the employee and the problem at hand. Review your earlier findings. Probe to see that you haven't missed something or that things haven't changed. Could a recent relocation or job assignment have created a different set of motivation problems? Check to see that the premise on which you are proceeding is sound; verify that you and employee are on the same page. Do the "three-beliefs" ratings still stand up? Would the employee answer today as he did earlier to the key questions, "Can I do the job (B-1)? Will outcomes be tied to my performance (B-2)? Will the outcomes be satisfying to me (B-3)?" Solutions based on faulty information are no solutions at all.

There is but one way to address difficult, seemingly intractable problems, that's *head-on*. This means being *open and honest with employees and not giving up on solving the problem.* As simple as that sounds, it is not. How would you handle this situation, for example? An employee wants an outcome very badly, but the manager has no control over giving it. (e.g. The company is being acquired, budgets are frozen and the employee wants a much-deserved raise.) No problem being open and honest here, right? Just tell the employee you're sorry, but there's nothing you can do. It's out of your hands . . . Only that's wrong; there very likely are things a manager can do, as we will explain in this chapter. The important point here is that the manager can't give up on solving the problem so easily.

The Belief System approach to solving

extraordinary motivation and performance problems is a two part exercise in managerial perseverance. The parts are (1) leveling and (2) giving the problem to the employee to solve. Let's get familiar with each.

STEPS IN HANDLING DIFFICULT PROBLEMS
- Level with the employee
- Give problem to employee

Leveling

Tell it like it is. Level with people, tell them honestly and exactly how things are; that's the origin of the term "leveling." It is the critical first step in the process of remedying difficult motivation and performance problems. Obviously, there will be times when employees will not want to hear what must be said, but the bedrock of reality must be found, albeit tactfully, before a solution can be constructed that will stand.

There are at least six situations that qualify as "difficult motivation and performance problems" in the Belief System scheme of things. The first two are tougher than the others because the manager has no control over the outcomes, i.e., cannot give what the employee wants, in the first instance; or keep the employee from getting something not wanted, in the second (more on this later). Here are the "tough half-dozen:"

1. Employees are performing well but they want

something *specific* that you cannot give them. This is a *trust (B-2) problem*. Leveling can go like this:

Leveling:
"I know you are interested in moving up in the company as soon as possible. We have reached a point where there simply are not any promotion opportunities available. I want to talk with you about why this has happened and discuss some things we can do until the opportunities reappear."

2. Employees *generally* are not getting outcomes that their performance warrants, and you can do nothing about it. This is a *trust (B-2) problem.*

Leveling:
"I know you are upset about being a top performer and not getting rewarded for it. To be honest with you, this isn't likely to change any time soon due to the company's current financial situation. With that said, I would like for us to put our heads together on this and see if we can figure out something that will make you happy."

3. Employees are performing well but are getting something they dislike, and you can do nothing about it. This is a *satisfaction (B-3) problem.*

Leveling:

"I want to thank you for making me aware that you do not like the kind of work you are doing now. At the same time I want to level with you and point out that I don't see any opportunity for that to change in the near future. Let me tell you why, and then we can discuss what this all means."

4. Employees think they deserve more, but their performance does not warrant it. This is a *trust (B-2) problem.*

Leveling:

"You recently expressed concern about the way you are rewarded here. I will be glad to review production records with you and the guidelines used for determining rewards. If you have been treated unfairly, I'll do what I can to straighten it out."

5. Employees have been getting by with poor performance and assume they can continue to do so. *This is a trust (B-2) problem.*

Leveling:

"This isn't the first time we have discussed your performance. I've made a mistake in the past by not working more closely with you to get it up to where it should be. My plan now is to work with you in whatever way I can to get this situation back on track. I think that together, you and I can devise a plan that will produce the results required of the job."

6. Employees simply are not qualified for the job. This is a *confidence (B-1) problem.*

Leveling:
"We have been discussing this situation for a long time now, and I think it has become apparent to both of us that the position you are in is not a good match for you. If we are in agreement on this, I would like for us to work together and hopefully come up with some options that will make sense for both of us."

Clearly, this is sensitive stuff. Handled wrong, it can go painfully awry, but not to handle it at all is worse. This is why the surest, safest approach is openness, honesty and exactitude. It is tough to refute the truth, particularly when it is *nicely expressed* and coupled with a clear *willingness to search out a good solution.* Those are the important qualifiers—"nicely expressed" (i.e., tactful, non-threatening, sensitive, etc.) and "let's find a better way" (i.e., "I'm not hear to fire you, but to help you").

Giving Problems To Employees

Bring employees into the search for ways out of difficult motivation and performance problems, give them the problem to solve—this is the real key to success. In order to do this, most managers must make a crucial transition: they must abandon the traditional belief that "It's my job to solve problems, that's what they pay me for," and recognize that employees are the best source of solutions to the problems that effect them.

Leveling precedes the process of "giving the problem to the employee." It goes something like this:

> ***Manager:***
> *Leveling*
> "I know you want that raise and, certainly, you deserve it. But my hands are tied. We are in the critical stage of the merger and acquisition, budgets are frozen and there's just no money . . . I don't want you to harbor any false hopes about that . . . ."
>
> *Giving Problem To Employee*
> "But I don't want to leave it at that. Help me to see if there is something else we can do that will make you feel better, something I have control over . . . ."

Now comes the relegation of responsibility for solving the problem—the employee, with the help and support of the manager, takes up the task. To see how this works, let's "give the employee" two of the most difficult motivation problems to befall managers.

DIFFICULT PROBLEMS

Problem 1   An employee believes "I will *not get* the outcome if I perform well (B-2) and it is something *I want* (B-3)," and the manager has no control over giving it. This is a B-2 problem.

Problem 2   An employee believes "I *will get* the outcome if I perform well (B-2) but it is something *I don't want* (B-3)," and the manager can't keep the employee from getting it. This is a B-3 problem.

Fundamentally different, each problem is handled differently. The Belief System provides three special tools for helping manager and employee to solve these particular problems. Let's look at these tools in context of the problems.

Problem 1

Substitution and *preference shifting* are the tools to employ when trying to fix the first major motivation problem—someone believes "*If I perform well, I will not get something I want*" (the B-2 problem).

TOOLS FOR SOLVING
DIFFICULT PROBLEM 1

("If I perform well, I will not get something I want.")

- Substitution
- Preference Shifting

Substitution—This is a technique aimed at substituting available outcomes that are acceptable to the employee for the desired outcomes that are not available. The employee may still prefer the desired outcome but compensating balances are often found in attractive substitutes.

The manager tries to accomplish two things: find substitute outcomes to compensate for the desired outcome the employee is not going to get, <u>and</u> find substitutes that are within the manager's control to give. The idea is to get the employee to kick around the possibilities; very likely, what he or she comes up with may not have occurred to the manager. Literally, the manager would hope for a list of things that the employee says would salve his or her wounds and diffuse the problem. The process might go like this:

Manager:

Giving Problem To Employee

"Let's explore some possibilities that might get you over the disappointment of the current promotion stalemate. A promotion may not be

> the only route to the things you want. Some
> other options may be attractive to you. I'm
> willing to work with you on this, but I need
> your help . . . ."

It is interesting that when managers start probing in this manner, solutions begin to materialize where before there seemed none. The manager's job is to get the employee to identify attractive outcomes that would serve as *substitutes* for the outcome that is desired but not available, a promotion in this case. It can be as simple as asking, "What are some things you want but are not now getting?" This question can be phrased many ways. In the context of the promotion situation, the question translates like this:

> *Manager:*
> "What is it about a promotion that is really
> attractive to you?"

> *Employee:*
> "A lot of things, I guess. For one thing, I
> would have more responsibility. There would
> be a greater opportunity for growth and
> development . . . More authority, more money,
> and greater exposure to some of the key
> people in the organization. That's important to
> me. I want a chance to show people what I can
> do . . . ."

Ask employees what they want, and in almost

every instance, they will tell you. *Asking* always works better than *telling*, or even *suggesting*. In this example, the employee identified six desirable outcomes. The manager's job then becomes, "Which ones can I give?" The openings for giving substitute outcomes appear in a variety of ways—once you have learned what is appealing to the employee. Here is one possibility.

> ### *Manager:*
> "Your comments are interesting. Our department has just been asked to do a special project for the vice president. He wants us to do a feasibility study on the possible expansion of our operation. I need a project leader. It wouldn't involve more money, but it is an opportunity to learn a lot. You'd have a small team working for you, and several of our key executives would have to be interviewed. A lot of responsibility is involved here and it definitely is a chance to show the right people what you can do. This isn't a promotion, but in a lot of ways, it may be even better. What do you think?"

There could be little doubt about the employee's reaction to this opportunity. It has multiple outcomes that collectively are more than an adequate substitute for a promotion in the short term. So when you find yourself confronting a *Problem 1* problem—"I will not

C H A P T E R   4

get the outcome (promotion) if I perform well (B-2), and it is something I want (B-3)"—turn to substitution for relief.

Preference shifting—Preference shifting is used when an employee is "hung up" on getting an outcome that appears to be more desirable than it really is. Sometimes employees want something, only to find out upon getting it, that the object of their desire is not so appealing as anticipated. In cases like these, the manager is advised to employ the technique of preference shifting. The objective is to shift the employee's preference *away* from the desired, albeit overestimated, outcome and thus remove it as an obstacle to the person's motivation and performance.

With preference shifting, first, level with the employee, then get the employee thinking toward a more thorough and objective view of the desired outcome. The manager's role is simply to help the employee to see the outcome more realistically, to recognize the negatives of a promotion as well as the positives, for example. Once employees begin to see the whole picture, their preference for the unavailable outcome usually begins to wane.

Managers must take care not to pressure employees to shift their preferences. The proper role is that of a facilitator, not the decision maker. Allow employees the opportunity of their own discovery, the chance to draw their own conclusions.

The following scenario gives a *Problem 1* problem

to the employee to solve and illustrates the use of preference shifting in removing the obstacle to the employee's motivation and performance.

Manager:
Giving Problem To Employee

"Having the door closed on something you really want is disappointing. There are a lot of ways to react when you realize the promotion you want is not possible. I can't tell you what to do or where to go from here. That's your decision, but I can help you think through this if you want me to."

The manager has thrown the preference shifting ball to the employee. It is in the right hands. Preference shifting can't be forced. It works only when the employee is willing to explore. Give the problem to the employee to solve, do it the right way, and you can stimulate a willingness to explore that can pay off handsomely for all concerned. When the employee starts asking questions, you are on the right track.

Employee:
"What do you mean? How can thinking through this problem make a difference for the better?"

Manager:
"Well, we've discussed those things about the

promotion that are attractive to you, but what about the negatives? Have you considered that side of it?"

Employee:
"Not really. What could be negative about a promotion?"

Manager:
"Let's look at the job in all its dimensions. There is going to be more responsibility, increased expectations, working nights and weekends, pressure to perform, endless streams of problems, stress, traveling two or three days a week, time away from the family, possible relocation, not to mention that downsizing hits middle management first and heaviest. That's the reality of the job just as much as the upside."

Employee:
"All that comes with the promotion I've had my eye on?"

Manager:
"Yes, but don't just take my word for it. Have you talked to any of the managers at that level now?"

Employee:
"No, but I've seen what's happened to some of them. They don't have any balance in their

lives. I'm not interested in that. Maybe it's best to hang onto what I have now, and worry about a promotion later on."

Helping employees with a more accurate assessment of the situation enables them to discover what really is important. The key is for the employee to make the discovery. For that person snagged on a desired outcome that has become an obsession, a do-or-die proposition that blocks motivation and performance, preference shifting can be a gentle and effective hand around the obstruction.

Problem 2

Offsets and *preference shifting* are designed to help correct the second big motivation problem—someone believes *"If I perform well, I will get something I do not want"* (the Belief-3 problem).

TOOLS FOR SOLVING DIFFICULT PROBLEM 2

("If I perform well, I will get something I don't want.")

- Offsets
- Preference Shifting

Offsets—For undesired outcomes that cannot be avoided, offset the dissatisfaction with available outcomes that outweigh the negatives. The person may not like the undesired outcome any more, but the offsets can compensate for the disappointment.

Here too, level with the employee, then explore the possibilities of offsets. The manager is simply searching the employee's thoughts for things that will offset the dissatisfaction with the outcomes the employee is unavoidably getting. Outcomes like these: the more successful the salesperson, the more she has to travel; the better the work done for a client, the more demanding he becomes; the more valuable one's input, the more meetings he has to attend. Solving problems like this runs the risk of throwing the baby out with the bath water. The best bet is to try to outweigh the bad with *additional good*; offset the unwanted outcomes with a willingness to make the person's life easier where you can. Offsetting may not boost motivation like the removal of the unwanted outcome, but it is better than doing nothing. The effort shows that you are aware of the problem and are doing your best to resolve it. The "thought counts," in this instance; with some employees, it counts a lot.

Helping employees with the "offsetting" option can evolve like this:

> ***Manager:***
> *Leveling*
> "I know you don't like doing the monthly reports, and I want to be honest about it with you. Unfortunately, there isn't anything we can do to change that right now."

Giving Problem To Employee

"Let's not just leave it at that, however. Although you are stuck with the reports, maybe there is something we can do to make it easier for you to live with. You're in a better position to determine that than I am. Any suggestions?"

In giving the problem to the employee, the manager is searching for outcomes the employee wants but is not getting. Those outcomes become possible offsets, i.e., outcomes that potentially are satisfying enough to offset the dissatisfaction from undesired outcomes the employee is unavoidably getting. As the employee mentions possible "offsetting outcomes," the manager will be tuned in particularly to those that are within his or her authority to give.

Employee:

"I'm always interested in learning new things. Our HR Department is offering a computer training class next month. I'd love to attend and sharpen my computer skills. Doing things like that now and then makes it easier to live with parts of the job I don't like. And with the computer class, I might get some ideas for doing the monthly reports faster. That would solve my problem. The way it is now, the reports take so much time I can't get my other work done . . . ."

Employees usually know what will solve their own problems. Managers who get in the habit of asking them for solutions get ahead of the game. Offsets are an excellent way to overcome *Problem 2* problems where an employee is getting unwanted outcomes (B-3); and asking the employee is the best way to find offsets that work.

Preference shifting—Preference shifting applies in *Problem 2* situations where an employee receives an outcome that seems more unappealing than it really is. Sometimes employees acquire a strong dislike for certain outcomes simply because they are not aware of the full implications. The goal in this situation is to shift the employee's preference to *liking* the *undesired* outcome. Fat chance, you say? Maybe not.

There are many occasions when employees view outcomes with dissatisfaction even though they actually offer things very desirable. Here are a few examples:

- An employee thought a temporary assignment in the marketing department not only was a waste of time, but was holding her back. Then she realized that she was being prepared for a pending restructuring of her job, and was not becoming a victim of downsizing.
- Performing well landed an employee in a special training program that was hard work and not very interesting. This wasn't the kind

of reward the employee was hoping for until he learned the program was exclusively for young managers on the fast track to promotion.

• The addition of more work when her plate was already full wasn't very encouraging to the young assistant until she discovered that "passing the test" would mean more responsibility and more money.

Preference shifting can work wonders for those employees struggling under the misperception that certain outcomes are more undesirable than they really are. Utilization of the technique calls for the manager to lead the employee through the process of self-discovery. Provide information as necessary to help the person fully understand the implications of the outcome. Asking questions rather than telling or suggesting is the best way to lead employees to a more complete and accurate understanding of outcomes. Well guided, employees often shift from viewing outcomes as dissatisfying to seeing them as desirable.

The manager's best course of action after "giving the problem to the employee," whether it's *Problem 1* or *Problem 2*, will depend on the employee's response. If there is a show of interest in "preference shifting," the manager will want to help develop a solution along that track. If it's the "substitution" of one outcome for another, or "offsetting" outcomes,

C H A P T E R   4

the manager chips in with assistance accordingly.

In times of "downsizing" where few promotions are available, pay raises are hard to come by, and job security is uncertain, it is absolutely imperative that managers search employees' hearts and minds for alternative ways to keep them satisfied and motivated.

The Rewards For Trying

Notice that in the preceding examples, the manager gives the problem to the employee and keeps it there. While supportive and helpful, the manager does not take the problem back from the employee. This is important. But let's face it, manager and employee can't always find good solutions to tough motivation problems no matter how diligent the effort. So all's for nought, the employee's dissatisfied, motivation's down and performance is headed the same way . . . Is that it? Is that the upshot of the manager's hard work and good intentions? Quite the contrary, we have found. Employees who have watched Belief System managers try and fail to remedy motivation problems overwhelmingly report a considerable liking for the attempt and the way it was done. Here is the reasoning:

- At least my manager *listened* to me.
- My manager obviously *cared* enough to go the "whole nine yards" to solve the problem.

HANDLING DIFFICULT PROBLEMS

- My manager *showed respect* for me by soliciting my opinion on how best to solve the problem.
- There was obvious *concern* on the manager's part for my welfare.

It turns out that employees receive satisfying outcomes (B-3) even though no solutions are found for their problems; the process itself gives valued outcomes by the very act of trying to find acceptable solutions.

Last Resort

But wait, there's one last tactic that may bring forth a solution when all else has failed . . . that's *leveling bold*. Here, you go beyond the basic message conveyed in the leveling step described previously, i.e., "You have a performance problem, I do not know what the solution is, maybe you can come up with some final suggestions, and I am willing to help you via preference shifting, substitution and offsets." Leveling bold says: "You have a performance problem, neither of us has come up with a workable solution, and I am not willing to live with the problem any longer." "Shape up or ship out" is the message. Cruel? It certainly doesn't have to be. It is not a message to be expressed in anger, but in kindness and concern for the employee. After all, leveling bold is based on the belief that employees should be given a final opportunity to take control of the situation and preserve their job if they want to do so. What more could employees expect than a chance to control their own destiny?

Furthermore, leveling bold is only employed when all other efforts have failed, so the message should come as no surprise to the person involved. The key with this approach is what is said and how it is said. Here is a right way:

> *Manager:*
> "Given what you want, and my knowledge of the situation here, I honestly don't believe we will ever be able to meet your needs, certainly not in the foreseeable future. You have a lot of capabilities. However, your performance is unacceptable. Have you considered other opportunities that might suit you better?"

No conscientious manager wants to come to this last resort, but, if your career is long, come to it you certainly will.

Summary

Difficult problems are more likely to be solved when employees share with management the responsibility for solving them. The sharing is achieved via a two-step process. The first step is *leveling* with the employee—the manager does not have a solution to the problem but he is willing to work with the employee to come up with one that is mutually acceptable. The second step is to *give the problem to the employee* while continuing to provide guidance along three proven problem-solving tracks. The tracks are (1) *shift preferences* away from outcomes that are not available or towards outcomes that are available, (2) find *substitutes* for outcomes that are desired but can't be had, and (3) find desirable outcomes to *offset* undesired outcomes that must be lived with. Go to the *leveling bold* option as a last resort.

82

C H A P T E R   5

Putting It All Together

To this point, you have learned the theoretical basis of the Belief System Of Motivation And Performance (chapter one), you have learned how to identify motivation and performance problems (chapter two), how solutions flow from an understanding of the causes of problems (chapter three) and how to handle particularly difficult situations (chapter four); now it is time to put it all together in the workplace. The principles and methods learned previously are but custom-made tools laying around on a job site with no one to put them in play. Without a craftsman, they build nothing. You, the manager, are the craftsman. Having learned the use for the tools, you must pick them up and go to work. That's what this chapter is about, wielding the tools provided you to forge a more productive workplace.

PUTTING IT ALL TOGETHER

Putting it all together comes down to a *diagnostic interview*, a face-to-face meeting of manager and employee to collaboratively arrive at solutions to performance problems that are acceptable to both parties. Throughout this book, we have implored you to *ask the employee* when there is a performance problem to be solved; this is where you do the asking.

There is much about the diagnostic interview that is familiar to those in managerial positions, and there is one thing that is quite different. The familiar is the practice of diagnosis itself; it is, afterall, basic to any discipline that seeks to remedy problems. In medicine, for example, no doctor would prescribe a medication or procedure for a condition he had not yet determined. Unfortunately, that is not always true in the management field: remedies are *normally* advanced for performance problems that have not been accurately or fully diagnosed. This is where the Belief System's diagnostic interview is critically different. The very heart of the process is the "belief diagnosis," the determination of a person's B-1, B-2 and B-3 beliefs. With the information gleaned from this unique communication, the manager knows the problem he is dealing with and its causes to an extent unobtainable any other way. Thus prepared, the manager is much more apt to succeed in his search for a good way out of an employee's performance problem.

How is a diagnostic interview conducted? The

three-part process is simple and effective, all of it designed to prepare for and proceed from the belief diagnosis.

The Diagnostic Interview Process		
Prepare for the Belief Diagnosis	**Diagnose the Three Beliefs**	**Solve the Belief Problem(s)**
• Document the employee's performance	• Rate Belief-1	• Ask employee for solutions
	• Rate Belief-2	• Agree on solution(s)
• Meet with the employee and state your performance concern	• Rate Belief-3	• Get and give a commitment
• Mutually agree that perform-ance is a problem		• Establish follow-up
		• Give positive reinforcement

Managers conduct diagnostic interviews, employing the tools of the Belief System, but employees are far from passive players. Indeed, the entire process, including the Belief System itself, is *employee centered.* Everything is founded in the proposition that employees should be equal partners with the manager when it comes to solving motivation and performance problems. So managers will be calling upon employees to (1) help diagnose the problems that are adversely affecting them and (2) help develop mutually acceptable solutions. This approach to problem-solving has proven highly effective for three reasons:

- Employees typically know more about their own performance problem than anyone else. It is their problem, after all.
- Employees generally know what will solve their problem. Since they live with the problem, you can bet that they have been thinking about how to solve it. They know what will work for them.
- Employees have *preferred* ways of solving problems they face. *Keep this in mind: a second best solution that an employee will accept is better than the best solution that causes resistance.*

The manager's role in the diagnostic interview is to gather information. That means "encourage the employee to talk," usually 80 percent of the time, or the process will fail. The manager guides the conversation with Belief System questioning, then "clams up" to hear and to interpret what is said. This—clamming up and paying close, unbiased attention to responses—is perhaps the most difficult of Belief System techniques for managers to master. Obviously, it can be done, and when it is, major breakthroughs in employee motivation often follow. We see it time and again.

Let's go through the diagnostic interview process step by step. First, the preparatory phase:

C H A P T E R 5

Document Employee Performance

Before meeting with the employee, gather specific information to document performance. Be prepared to show the employee that actual performance is not meeting performance expectations. Be specific whenever possible. Examples of instances where performance has been a problem are helpful. Try to pinpoint symptoms of the problem. Give some thought to what may be causing them. Some things can be fairly obvious with a little Belief System thinking: if the employee recently came from a bankrupt firm that promised much for performance but could not deliver, it could easily be that the person still believes that "Outcomes will not be tied to my performance." A B-2 problem, perhaps? Just remember this: it is impossible to resolve employee performance problems if you cannot convincingly illustrate where the employee falls short of established standards. Do your homework.

State Your Performance Concern

Now face-to-face with the employee, indicate your concern about motivation and performance. Point out why you are concerned. Be direct and to the point. When doing this, show concern. This is no time for accusations or a threatening manner. Exhibit a desire to help, not to punish. Here are some ways to do this.

• "Your monthly call reports show a worrisome

decline in sales activity over the last two months. With your sales performance down, I thought we had better talk. Between the two of us, we ought to be able to get things back on track . . . ."

- "There appears to be a breakdown in communication between you and the marketing department. Good teamwork is critical here if we are to meet delivery schedules. I want to see what you and I can do to open up the flow of information . . . ."

After opening statements like that to explain the purpose of the meeting, stop and wait for the employee to respond. This is step one in getting employees involved in solving their own motivation and performance problems. An employee may be hesitant the first time you approach a problem this way. Be patient. Offer encouragement. Don't let the employee get by with comments like, "Oh, gee, I didn't know anything was wrong." Responses like that usually indicate a reluctance to talk. Try to eliminate the reluctance with a sincere expression that you want to help.

Agree That Performance Is A Problem

No progress will occur unless both you and the employee agree that there is a performance problem. There should also be understanding and agreement on the disparity between *actual* and *expected* performance. This is where the manager's homework comes in handy. It does no good to say, "Your performance hasn't been up to par," unless you can justify your remarks. So don't be vague, be prepared with details of what has brought you to the diagnostic interview.

The Beliefs Diagnosis

Phase two of the diagnostic interview process involves the actual diagnosis of the employee's "three beliefs" as described in chapter one—Belief-1, "Can I do the job?" Belief-2, "Will the outcomes be tied to my performance?" Belief-3, "Will the outcomes be satisfying to me?" In the Belief System approach to motivation, the beliefs diagnosis is where the "rubber meets the road." For in the interface of manager and employee is the interface of problem and solution. The motivation problem resides in the employee, he or she is the one that is not performing; the solution to the problem probably also resides in the employee, though he or she may not understand that it does. It makes no difference whether the employee understands or not, however, for employees can do little or nothing to solve their own problem without the manager's intercession. Unless a trained manager creates the right environment for a solution to emerge, the problem and solution lie fallow in the vessel of the employee. A Belief System manager can turn up that vessel and shake out a solution that will take root to the benefit of all.

So once agreement has been reached that, yes, there is a performance problem and, yes, manager and employee generally agree on its specifics, move into the "three beliefs" diagnosis. Use the rating scales to log what you learn. As always in the diagnostic process, ask questions and listen, remember the questions to be answered. Here is an important tip: *diagnose all three beliefs.* Don't find a

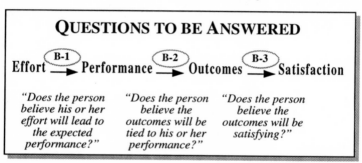

QUESTIONS TO BE ANSWERED

Effort ⟶ Performance ⟶ Outcomes ⟶ Satisfaction
(B-1)   (B-2)   (B-3)

"Does the person believe his or her effort will lead to the expected performance?"

"Does the person believe the outcomes will be tied to his or her performance?"

"Does the person believe the outcomes will be satisfying?"

problem at B-1 or B-2 and stop. You may have more than one belief problem on your hands. Here is how a beliefs diagnosis might unfold:

Manager:

"Is there anything I can do to help you solve the problem?"

Employee:

"I don't know. With all the recent changes in procedures, I've really gotten confused about things." (Sounds like a Belief-1 problem.

Cause: not knowing what to do and/or how to do it.)

Manager:
"Can you give me an example of what you mean?"

Employee:
"All those new procedures from the engineering department . . . A lot of us had trouble understanding them. The staff meeting was short on explanation, and we didn't get any training." (Solutions are implied here.)

Manager:
"Anything else?" (Don't stop with discovery of the B-1 problem; there may be others at B-2 or B-3.)

Employee:
"Not really. It was smooth sailing until all the changes. I was knocking out the work . . . Now I'm having trouble getting things done right and on time. It's not a good feeling."

When the diagnosis is completed, summarize your understanding of the problem. This gives the employee a chance to confirm the diagnosis, or to make corrections or additions. The summary should be a brief restatement of Belief-1, Belief-2, and Belief-3, including the causes mentioned by the employee. Nothing else is necessary or desirable. There is no need for explanation or justification, criticism or sympathy, lectures or finger pointing, being defensive or offensive, or offering suggestions or solutions. Just summarize the diagnosis. Then wait for employee feedback to be sure you have summarized the problem correctly. Here is an example.

Manager:

"So what you're saying is that even if you work hard, you can't do the kind of job you want to do because you don't fully understand all the new procedures." (The employee is saying "I can't do it." Cause: the new procedures.)

Employee:

"You've hit it right on the head." (Now you have a good idea of the employee's Belief-1 level—low—and you know the cause.)

Ask Employee For Solutions

With the beliefs diagnosis in hand, the manager is uniquely prepared to move into the critical third phase of the diagnostic process: developing solutions to motivation and performance problems. It begins with the manager *asking the employee for solutions.* Then comes the hard part for many managers. Hold any ideas you may have for solving the problem. Instead, let the employee offer solutions. There is no intent to curry favor here, making employees feel good is secondary to a higher objective—finding real, effective solutions to real, debilitating problems. No manager has all the answers to employee motivation problems; employees do have answers for their own problems. Some employees will be eager to tell you. Others will not. If they seem reluctant, encourage them. Employees always have ideas about how to solve their own motivation problems. You, the manager, may not agree with the solution, but you are advised to ask. Keep asking until the message is clear, "I really would like and value *your* ideas for solving the problem." Do not give your ideas first. This is tempting when the employee is hesitant, but resist the urge. Try something like this:

> *Manager:*
> "What do you think is the best way to handle this?"
>
> *Employee:*
> "I'm not sure. What do you think?" (Resist the temptation to field the question with an answer.)
>
> *Manager:*
> "You're good at figuring out things like this. I would really be interested in what you think we should do?"

PUTTING IT ALL TOGETHER

Employee:
"I just need somebody to go over the procedures with me. I know where I'm confused, I know what to ask."

Manager:
"Do you have anybody in mind to help you?"

Employee:
"I hit it off pretty good with Bob, one of the engineers that developed the new procedures. I'd feel comfortable working with him."

Manager:
"How much time are we talking about?"

Employee:
"Probably getting together for an hour or so, two or three times would be enough."

Manager:
"Anything other than the time with Bob?"

Employee:
"No, that should do it."

End this segment of the discussion by summarizing the employee's suggestions. The purpose is to be sure you understand the key points the employee is making. It is a fatal mistake to seek out solutions, then move ahead with a misunderstanding of what the employee said. Summarizing is the best check against that happening.

C H A P T E R   5

Agree On A Solution

Sometimes the solution recommended by an employee will be completely satisfactory to you, the manager. If so, indicate agreement and move on to the next step. When the solution isn't acceptable, what do you do? If the snags are minor, try this:

- Posing questions about the things that concern you often helps an employee see the wisdom of an alternative solution. For example . . .

  Manager:
  "Let me get this straight. You want to start work at 6:30 in the morning and finish the day by 2:30? What are you going to do about engineering support? Bob doesn't come in until 8:45."

  Employee:
  "Oh, I see what you mean. Flex-time isn't going to work in this case."

Determine some options, then settle on one that suits both of you.

- Point out what you are concerned about and why. Ask for alternatives. Get the employee's opinion. By focusing on why an alternative is in the best interest of the employee, you likely will find that the employee is inclined to agree with you.

What if the employee's solution is simply too far off base? This will happen sometimes. What is to be done?

- Option one is to ask the employee for any other ideas for dealing with the problem. Keep asking in hopes that an acceptable solution surfaces. If it does, come to agreement on its acceptability.
- Option two is to pose questions about the proffered solution that reveal the difficulties with adopting it. For example, "How would you go about implementing this?" Or, "How do you think our customers (other employees, management, etc.) will react to this?" Or, "Can we do this given our time, cost, and manpower constraints?"
- Option three is to point out the flaws in the solution, doing so as tactfully as possible. Offer suggestions for overcoming them, and solicit the employee's reaction to the recommendations.

One of the three will normally work. Try all three options if necessary.

Get and Give A Commitment

Once agreement is reached on the best solution to a performance problem, it is vital that both parties

C H A P T E R   5

make a commitment: the employee to solve the problem, the manager to help the employee. Here is the procedure. First, summarize the solution agreed to. Get the employee to accept the responsibility for its success and to make a commitment to implement the solution. State what the employee is to do, and what you are committed to do. Here is an example.

> *Manager:*
> "Let me see if I've got this right. You want to meet with Bob two or three times for an hour or so each time?"
>
> *Employee:*
> "That should do it."
>
> *Manager:*
> "Do you think this will get your performance up where it should be?"
>
> *Employee:*
> "Yes, I think it will solve the problem. I'll certainly dig in to make it work." (This is the employee's commitment.)
>
> *Manager:*
> "O.K., I'll talk with Bob and have him get in touch with you to set up a time for the first meeting." (This is the manager's commitment.)

PUTTING IT ALL TOGETHER

Establish Follow-up

A commitment from both sides to take action is not the end of the process. How will efforts to solve the problem be monitored? What kind of follow-up will be done by both the manager and the employee. This must be decided in the diagnostic interview process. Here is an illustration of how it might work:

> ### *Manager:*
> "There are a couple of things I want you to do. First, let me know when you and Bob have set a time to get together. Second, after the first meeting between you two, let's get together and discuss how the meeting went, and see if you still think this approach is going to get your performance back up to where it needs to be."

Give Positive Reinforcement

How you end the one-on-one discussion is very important. To give the effort every opportunity to succeed, send the employee off to his or her appointed rounds in the best frame of mind possible.

- Thank the employee for participating in the diagnostic process.
- Positively reinforce everything the employee did in the meeting that you would like to see repeated in future discussions. Examples include the person's willingness to talk

openly and honestly, to help in figuring out
what to do to solve the problem and being
concerned about improving performance.
The closing comments may go like this:

Manager:
"One more thing. Thanks! I'm glad to have
you working here. You're always concerned
about doing a good job and I appreciate your
willingness to work this thing out."

The thanks expressed by employees for the
managerial manner just described often surprises new
adherents to the Belief System of motivation and
performance. Instead of the usual one-sided "critique
of authority," employees find Belief System
managers well prepared to address the problem at
hand and legitimately interested in helping to reach
mutually acceptable solutions. The effect on
motivation and performance is usually apparent in
short order.

Summary

The key to "putting it all together"—the principles
and devices of the Belief System—is the beliefs
diagnosis. It gently forces an accurate diagnosis of
problems and causes, and substantially increases the
prospects of finding good solutions to performance
short-falls. The key to diagnosing and solving
motivation problems quickly is to put the ball in the

employee's court. Rely on employees to help diagnose problems and to come up with solutions. It takes information to solve problems; and when it comes to motivation problems, employees have the information managers need to make good decisions. Using the employee-centered approach recommended here will work. You can make it work for you.

C H A P T E R   6

Questions and Answers

Where to from here? We have introduced you to the Belief System Of Motivation And Performance, explained something of its workings and how it applies in the workplace. But we have probably raised as many questions as we have answered. Let us now answer some of the logical questions that come to mind when anyone is so bold as to propose a solution to problems as pervasive as those dealing with motivation and performance.

The first question *ought* to be, "How do I know that the Belief System is all that it is proclaimed to be?" *Has it been tested?* What's the track record? Other questions that we frequently hear are these:

- How do I get started with the Belief System?
- What kind of resistance to Belief System

training can I expect from my workforce? Are employees reluctant to use it? Are managers?

- What is the history of long-term utilization of Belief System training? Is it actually used or, like most training experiences, promptly forgotten after the instruction?
- The Belief System focuses on the manager-employee relationship, but does it have anything of value to offer at the organizational level?
- How does the Belief System relate to diversity?
- Can it be used in "team" development?
- The Belief System solves motivation and performance problems, but can it *prevent* them? Any other by-product benefits I ought to know about?

Now, some answers . . .

Has the Belief System been tested?

Yes. The Belief System is a work-in-progress since 1977. Every year has seen refinement and extension of the basic theoretical and application models. It is tried and proved time and again in the small, exclusive circle of clientele personally serviced by these authors. Not until 1991 was Dr. Green induced to take the Belief System beyond the scope of those consulting practices. That's when he was called into a consulting assignment at AT&T. The upshot of that experience, still in progress as of the publication of this book, was the development of an "implementation model" that *cascades* Belief System training down through entire organizations, top managers to hourly people, regardless of the size of the workforce. The program, prompted by William J. Barkley, Jr., Human Resources Vice President of AT&T, has exceeded all expectations. As Barkley stated, "The Belief System is doing nothing less than changing the way this organization does business."

The results of the AT&T experience have been very positive. Motivation and performance problems have been solved and potential problems have been prevented. The Belief System has had a strong impact on management styles and the motivation and performance of employees. The Belief System is making AT&T a better, more productive place to work, according to Bill Barkley and a succession of AT&T managers and direct-reports employing the Belief System. Published research studies that document the success of the Belief System at AT&T and other organizations are forthcoming.

How does one get started with the Belief System?

This book is a start. Other books on the subject offer additional insights (see list in back of book) . . . but the ability to fully employ the *Belief System Of Motivation And Performance* in the workplace begins with training. In the Belief System, manager and direct-reports are ideally trained *en masse,* as a team. Managers are taught to "share the responsibilities of management with their employees" and why it is a good idea. Employees learn how to "solve their *own* motivation and performance problems" and why it is in their best interest to do so. Organizational performance is raised on a philosophy rooted in the "individuality" of each employee.

What happens after Belief System training?

Two things. First, the manager and each of his or her direct-reports meet, one-on-one, for 3–4 hours in a systematic, carefully scripted problem-solving work session. Second, both parties "follow up" this meeting with a reminder program that assures that mutually-agreed upon solutions are implemented and Belief System training is firmly imbedded in the managerial philosophies of each trainee. Utilization of Belief System methodology does not stop when the training stops. Problems are actually solved and prevented.

Employees come to the one-on-one session prepared with solutions to specific motivation-performance problems previously identified. The solutions are the employees' own, formulated in a step-by-step *self-diagnosis* built upon the Belief System. The manager, too, assesses the problems in a *best-guess diagnosis* intended to clear away misperceptions he or she may harbor about the employees. Thus prepared, manager and employee follow the *Diagnostic Interview* process described in Chapter 5.

The primary tool for preventing motivation and performance problems is the *Belief System Profile*. It reveals the strengths and weaknesses of the employee's motivational beliefs (B-1, B-2, B-3), highlights existing and potential problems, and identifies logical solutions including "substitutions" and "offsets." It is most difficult for motivation and performance problems to take root in teams and organizations steeped in the Belief System.

PROGRAM DESCRIPTION

Training – The manager and his or her direct-reports meet to learn the Belief System methodology and how to use it.

Application – Manager meets individually with each direct-report, in the presence of a trained Belief System facilitator, to identify and remedy motivation and performance problems specific to that person. This occurs within 4–6 weeks of the conclusion of the training.

Follow-up – The Belief System is kept alive in manager and direct-reports with written commitments made one to the other, and a Reminder Guide that converts training to managerial philosophy.

QUESTIONS AND ANSWERS

What makes the one-on-one session so effective?

Here is what managers and employees tell us:

- Both manager and employee understand the intent of the Belief System and how it is suppose to work (a result of the training approach that teaches manager and direct-reports *together*).

- Both manager and employee prepare specifically for each segment of the one-on-one session, the preparation designed to foster understanding, appreciation and consensus.

- A structured, scripted process is followed in the one-on-one session that covers a lot of sensitive ground tactfully and effectively. Things stay on track, objectives are reached and good things happen.

- The presence of a trained "facilitator" is a decided plus. This unbiased third party, usually the trainer, keeps the session focused and on schedule, and contributes substantially to the success of the meeting.

- Managers and employees are *motivated* to make the one-on-one sessions work. Both win: employees get to solve their own motivation and performance problems, managers reap the rewards of happier, more productive employees.

Do motivation and performance problems actually get solved?

Absolutely, and here's why . . . The Belief System is anchored in the premise that employees know more about what's bothering them on the job and what it would take to solve the problem than any one else could possibly know. That's true, of course, but it means nothing without some effective means to bring the employee into the problem-solving process. The Belief System is designed specifically to that end. Managers actually follow a process that "gives the problem to the employee to solve." That same process equips the employee to actually accomplish what is being asked of him or her. And what better solution than one of your own creation, backed up and embraced by the boss?

Employees report that they feel comfortable with this kind of empowerment because Belief System training readies them for challenges and opportunities. Managers and employees alike tell us that the interplay of preparation and accountability, openness and honesty, sweeps away problems as nothing else does.

Is the Belief System really preventive?

Indeed it is. If you know what constitutes motivation, and if you have a practical way to effectively measure it, then you can detect motivation problems in people before performance begins to decline or before the decline reaches critical levels. Motivation problems often can be anticipated, and prevented from arising, once managers gain a thorough understanding of the motivational makeup of each individual employee. What is the source of this understanding? It comes from the employee during the *one-on-one* sessions. Managers trained in the Belief System know all that's needed to head-off performance problems caused by motivational shortcomings.

Are there other benefits derived from Belief System training?

Many managers and employees tell us that the benefits of Belief System training go beyond preventing and solving performance problems. Employees generally communicate more openly with their managers. Manager-employee relationships usually are strengthened. Though less directive, managers tend to become stronger and more effective as they rely increasingly on the capabilities of their employees. Employees become more accountable and display greater initiative when it comes to their own performance. Benefits like these lead managers and employees alike to believe that "this is a better place to work" (B-3).

Are employees reluctant to use the Belief System?

It depends. *Before* the one-on-one session, there is

anxiety and reluctance on the part of employee *and* manager. Employees, in particular, often don't want to engage in face-to-face discussions with their boss of the type prescribed by the Belief System. What if the manager takes what's said the wrong way? For being open and honest, a person could end up getting undesirable outcomes—the manager's resentment (a B-3 problem). Whose to say that the one-on-one session will work as devised? (A B-1 "confidence" problem.) And there is uncertainty about whether the one-on-one session will really change anything (a B-2 problem—"Will outcomes be tied to my performance?").

Indeed, if the one-on-one session was not *unavoidable,* there would likely be no critical meeting of the minds, no real solution to the problems that drag down performance of employee, manager and organization—and little use of the Belief System.

But *after* the one-on-one session, the doubts and anxieties evaporate. The system works, it yields results, and trainees are not reluctant to use it thereafter.

Do managers and employees continue using the Belief System?

Are people motivated to repeat what has proven successful? Yes, certainly. Consistently and unabashedly, managers and employees report real breakthroughs in motivation and performance levels after Belief System training. Success begets success. Practitioners of the Belief System approach to management gain confidence ("I can do the job expected of me"—B-1). They understand that "outcomes will be tied to their performance" (B-2) and that those "outcomes will be satisfying" (B-3). In other words, managers and employees continue using the Belief System long after training simply because they are *motivated* to do so.

What about applications beyond the manager-employee interface?

The Belief System can be the very core of typical organizational functions. Take *recruitment and selection,* for example. It behooves any organization to carefully match new hires with available job openings. That means a good bit more than simply finding people whose technical skills match the requirements of the job; it also means matching the pluses and minuses of the job with the motivational needs of the prospects. Otherwise, turnover occurs and performance suffers. Hire a person whose skill level far exceeds the demands of the job, for instance, and watch motivation and performance decline as that person realizes that the intrinsic outcomes of the job are not very satisfying (B-3). The Belief System Of Motivation and Performance, particularly the *Belief System Profile*, offers a better way to match new recruits with available jobs.

Training and development programs built on the Belief System produce more highly motivated employees which impacts positively on organizational performance. Entire organizations, like individuals, can have high or low B-1 levels ("we can or cannot do the job"), can suffer from pervasive B-2 problems ("outcomes are not tied to performance") or can labor under the heavy weight of B-3 afflictions ("the outcomes of the job are not satisfying").

Develop a workforce that believes "we can do it," and the organization is a leg up on better days. Develop an organization that "ties outcomes to performance" and to nothing else, and B-2 problems cease to be a drag. Develop enough employees who find the "outcomes of their work to be satisfying," and the organization is off and running.

Reward and incentive programs rooted in the Belief System take on new dimensions. Many organizations simply do not tie rewards to performance. Frequently, everyone is treated the same, or politics rules, or seniority, or plain old favoritism . . . Reward systems in environments like this are not very motivating because people conclude that "outcomes are not tied to performance (B-2), so why work harder or smarter?"

Employing the Belief System as the foundation for reward and incentive programs will produce the results desired—better performance.

These are but a few of the organizational functions that would benefit from the adoption of the Belief System approach to business.

How does the Belief System relate to diversity?

Everyone is different. Everyone knows that. Yet, modern management practice still clings to the age-old belief that you treat everyone the same. The Belief System says that you "manage to the individuality of the employee," whatever his or her race, gender, age, idiosyncrasies or other distinguishing features. The results of this simple principle are profound . . . .

Managers must get to know their people and vice versa. It is not so difficult because a system is provided to do it. With *understanding* comes *appreciation* of one another's differences, of the strengths and weaknesses of each member of the team. Knowing these things, a Belief System manager can make team diversity an asset. Employ individual strengths where they can produce the best results, bolster weaknesses with training and support, improve performance with the very differences that many assume to be a liability.

For all their differences, those from culturally diverse backgrounds differ none at all when it comes to performance on the job: they must believe that "I can do it," that "outcomes will be tied to my performance" and that "the outcomes will be satisfying." Diversity training built on the Belief System Of Motivation And Performance will generate rewards for all parties far beyond that achieved by diversity training alone.

How can the Belief System be used for team development?

Successful teams by definition "share a common goal." Unfortunately, team members typically don't have the same personal goals. Where the Belief System is used in planning and team development, we have witnessed an open and honest merging of team and individual goals. This occurs because the goals are discussed in the context of B-1 considerations, "Can the goals be reached? (Can we do it?); B-2 considerations, "What will we get if we succeed?" (Will outcomes be tied to performance?); and B-3 considerations, "Will we like it if we get it?" (Will the outcomes be satisfying?). The bottom-line is this: team development built on the Belief System brings into play all the talents and energies of the team. Performance can only go up.

What do we predict for the future of the Belief System?

It works. Motivation is improved in teams and organizations that use it, performance rises. In the present economic environment where the workforce is plagued by uncertainty and misgivings, the Belief

System touches and heals and strengthens in all the right places. Notwithstanding the technologies and sophistications woven into the modern workplace, the whole thing is still driven by people. With all their frailties and imperfections, people must still perform in order for organizations to perform.

So long as that is true, motivation cannot be overlooked or poorly dealt with. No other program deals with this critical issue with the thoroughness and effectiveness of the Belief System Of Motivation And Performance. So we believe the future of the Belief System to be bright. There is an urgent need in the workplace for what the Belief System offers. We believe that the market will find what it is looking for, particularly with your help. If you find the Belief System to be of value, perhaps you would spread the word. Together, we can help make the workplace a better place to spend the day and improve productivity and prosperity in the process.

Belief System Products and Services

For further information on the products and services that follow, please call 1-800 351-1626.

Belief System Development Program—A team development program that includes carefully orchestrated problem-solving sessions and a system for long-term follow-up and program utilization. Development manuals for employees and managers are included.

Belief System Profile—An instrument to measure the extent of employee motivation (B-1, B-2, B-3) for the jobs they do. Motivation problems that adversely effect performance are revealed. The Belief System Profile comes in an "employee" version, "manager", and "sales" version. A computer-generated analyses of the completed instrument is an optional part of the package.

Behavior Style Analysis—Based on the widely accepted DISC model of behavior development by William Marston and John Geier, this instrument is tailored to the problem-solving focus of the Belief System. Understand a person's natural behavioral style and you know (1) how best to work with that person and (2) what jobs best match his or her personality. Greater motivation and performance results. A computer analyses is an integral part of this program.

Preferred Motivation Environment—This instrument identifies the job environment that is most attractive to employees. The more closely the job and the atmosphere associated with the job matches what is motivating to an employee, the more motivated that employee becomes and the better he or she performs. The instrument is designed primarily for employees. A manager's version is principally a note-taking document for employee feedback.

The Self-Analysis—This is an instrument for employees to identify and solve motivation-performance problems that hinder them, in the opinion of the manager. The manager analyzes the same problems independently with the Best-Guess Diagnosis. The result is a manager and employee "on the same page," solving problems together, to the mutual benefit of both.

Belief System Reminder Guide—A follow-up system to ensure that promises made during the one-on-one problem-solving sessions are kept and that the Belief System is used long after the initial training ends.

Behavior Style Tendency Charts—Four charts, one for each basic behavioral style (High-D, High-I, High-S, High-C). Each chart lists those tendencies that characterize the particular behavior style and explains the best ways to work with people who exhibit that style.

Causes And Solutions Chart—A ready reference to specific motivation problems, their causes and logical solutions approach. With this tool, managers and employees trained in the Belief System can move more quickly and confidently through the process of identifying and solving debilitating motivation and performance problems.

Performance And Motivation Strategies For Today's Workforce—Hardback book by Thad Green, published by Quorum Books, 1992, 231 pages. This is the "bible" of Belief System methodology. In substantial detail, it defines the basic model that underlies the Belief System Of Motivation And Performance and shows how the model is applied in the real-world workplace. The book can be ordered direct from the publisher—1-800-225-5800.

The Belief System—Paperback book by Thad Green and Merwyn Hayes, published by Beechwood Press, 1993. The Belief System condenses, simplifies and expands upon the material presented in Thad Green's earlier book, Performance And Motivation Strategies For Today's Workforce. The book is "reader friendly" and captivating, according to several reviewers.

The Belief Cascade—A paperback in novel form, an allegorical account of a Belief System training session and all that typically goes on in these programs. Written by Thad Green and William J. Barkley, Jr., Vice President for AT&T. Publication date Spring 1994. The book is distinctive not only for its novelized format but for the highly effective "implementation" model that it introduces. *The Beliefs Cascade* shows the reader how Belief System training is "cascaded" down through larger organizations from top-most manager to hourly workers.

Developing and Leading the Sales Organization—Hardback book by Thad Green, published by Quorum Books, 1998, 242 pages. This book resulted from applying The Belief System Of Motivation And Performance in both large and small sales organizations. It shows that sales results improve when selling is viewed as motivating people to buy, and the motivation to sell is seen in a broader context than usual.

Motivation, Beliefs, And Organization Transformation— Hardback book by Thad Green and Raymond T. Butler, published by Quorum Books, 1999, 207 pages. This book relates the author's extensive experience in using The Belief System Of Motivation And Performance as a change model with individuals, teams, and organizations, including large-scale change efforts.

Motivation Management—Hardback book by Thad Green, published by Davies-Black Publishing, 2000, 268 pages. As an advocate for looking to employees and the best source for solutions to their motivation and performance problems, the author provides a wealth of real-world examples and all the tools a manager needs to open up channels of communication and transform the employee feedback process into a unique opportunity to set things right in the workplace.

About the Authors

Dr. Thad Green is a management consultant, writer and author based in Atlanta, Georgia. He is considered by many pundits in the management field to be the foremost authority on motivation and performance in the U.S. His other writings on the subject include the books, *Performance And Motivation Strategies For Today's Workforce* (1992, Quorum Books) and *The Beliefs Cascade* (co-authored by William J. Barkley, Jr., Vice President, AT&T; to be released in late 1994). Dr. Green has served on the management faculty at the University of Georgia, Auburn University, Mississippi State University and Emory University. As a consultant, he has worked with clientele like AT&T, Delta Air Lines, Holiday Inns, Outdoor Marine Corporation and many government agencies including the U.S. Department of Labor and Department of Agriculture.

Dr. Merwyn Hayes is the CEO and President of the Hayes Group International. He is an internationally respected authority on executive coaching and team development. A client recently described him this way: "Merwyn is able to get issues on the table and initiate openness without damaging our self esteem. He helps us leave planning sessions with greater clarity of where we are going and pleased to be working as a team." Organizations that have recently employed Dr. Hayes are the Federation of State Medical Boards, General Electric, International Paper, ABB, The South Financial Group, Cox Media, Wachovia, GKN Driveline, Augusta Newsprint, Curtiss Wright, the University of Utah Medical Center, Duke University Medical Center, and Westinghouse Energy Systems. Prior to leading the Hayes Group, Dr. Hayes was a University professor and administrator at the University of Illinois, University of Georgia, and the Babcock Graduate School of Management at Wake Forest University.